Treating Your Hyperactive and Learning Disabled Child

The New York Institute for Child Development, Inc., is a national, nonprofit center that specializes in the diagnosis and treatment of learning disabled, hyperactive, and underachieving children. It has been in existence for over ten years. The thrust of the institute's work is in the investigation of the biochemical, nutritional, and functional disorders that cause hyperactivity and learning disabilities and in the development of a unique treatment approach that combines sensorimotor exercises and nutrition management. The institute's method has proven to be highly successful.

Treating Your Hyperactive and Learning Disabled Child

WHAT YOU CAN DO

The New York Institute for Child Development, Inc. with Richard J. Walsh

CONTRIBUTING EDITORS
Lila Agree, R.D., M.A.
Darral Chapman, R.P.T.
Shaindy Gross, M.S.
Suzanne Van Nolde, M.A.
Judith I. Dowd
Jerome Vogel, M.D.

ANCHOR PRESS/DOUBLEDAY
GARDEN CITY, NEW YORK
1979

Library of Congress Cataloging in Publication Data

New York Institute for Child Development.
  Treating the whole child.

  Includes index.
    1. Children—Management. 2. Child development.
3. Hyperactive children. 4. Learning disabilities.
I. Walsh, Richard Joseph, 1926-   joint author.
II. Agree, Lila. III. Title.
HQ773.N48 1979   649'.1
ISBN: 0-385-12508-9
Library of Congress Catalog Card Number 76-23750

Contents

Foreword

In American society today, parents find themselves confronted with a variety of problems that weren't listed in their marriage vows. Not only are we often cut off from the child-rearing supports of relatives and neighbors, but we must now work our way through a maze of questions about health, education, and government that seem to have no sure or satisfying answers. At times we may spend weeks, months, and years in finding solutions to medical and educational problems involving our children.

This is painfully true when a child is hyperactive or has a learning problem or, as is usually the case, both. At the New York Institute for Child Development we constantly see families who have spent a great deal of time and money searching for answers. Letters coming to our office from all over the United States and Canada often start with the word *help!* Parents are frustrated and discouraged. The child's learning problems have led to poor self-image and often accompanying emotional problems. Fortunately we have been able to provide answers for many of these families and, most important, for their children.

The terms *hyperactivity* and *learning disabilities* describe subtle, seemingly nonorganic problems that interfere with a child's ability to learn, to read, to write, and to compute. Although these terms are descriptive of symptoms rather than of causes, they have gained wide acceptance. At least they have served to distinguish a population of normal children who are not otherwise physically or emotionally handicapped, so that we can focus on the causes of, and cures for, what is disturbing them.

It is unfortunate that, at the present time, despite the danger of harmful side effects and despite the fact that they do not help hyperactive children learn, drugs are the primary therapy used in treating between 1 and 2 million children annually in the United States. It is our fond hope that this book will change this practice and raise the level of understanding about the problem of hyperactivity and learning disabilities, which affects 15 to 20 per cent of American schoolchildren.

Treating Your Hyperactive and Learning Disabled Child was written for two basic reasons: to define the problem and to share the answers to the problem developed by the New York Institute for Child Development.

The New York Institute for Child Development, a national nonprofit center that specializes in the diagnosis and treatment of learning disabled, hyperactive, and underachieving children, was founded in 1968. One of the few centers in the country that believes physical imbalances are the basis for many learning disabilities, the New York Institute looks at children affected with these problems from a multidisciplinary perspective—physiologically, biochemically, neurologically, and developmentally.

Experience with thousands of children at the New York Institute for Child Development has shown that learning disabilities and hyperactivity may result from a variety of causes: neurological or functional difficulties, such as vision-perception problems or poor motor coordination; biochemical imbalances, such as food allergies; skipping stages in the developmental process, such as creeping or crawling; and malnutrition.

The standard treatments for learning disabled children have been traditional academic tutoring, which doesn't take into account physical or biochemical problems; drugs, which merely attack the symptoms, not the causes; and psychological counseling, which tends to treat a child's behavior without concern for physical diagnosis.

The New York Institute for Child Development's unique approach to learning disorders combines sensorimotor exercises and nutrition management, a process so effective that almost 90 per cent of children in therapy at the institute have been treated successfully.

The aim of this book is to enable parents of hyperactive and learning disabled children to understand that there are effective answers to these problems and to make them aware of how to find these answers.

JUDITH I. DOWD
Executive Director

I

The Nature
of the Problem

In the United States today, it is estimated that between 7 and 9 million school-age children of normal to high IQ suffer from hyperactivity and/or learning disabilities. The problem has grown to such proportions that the federal government enacted legislation in 1975 (Public Law 94-142) to extend the term *handicapped* to include those children who have specific learning disabilities. The law recognized the need for special attention and funding to be provided for them. Although the general public may be unaware of the extent of the problem of hyperactivity and learning disabilities in our society, the parents of these children know full well the pain and frustration they and their children suffer.

Not all learning disabled children are hyperactive, but almost all hyperactive children are learning disabled. A *learning disabled child* is a child of normal to even high intelligence who is unable to perform up to his potential in the basics of reading, writing, and arithmetic. The learning disabled child is not to be confused with the *slow learner*, who may need additional help but who can learn to perform. The federal government's definition specifies the following:

"Specific learning disability" means a disorder in one or more of the basic psychological processes involved in understanding or in using language, spoken or written, which may manifest itself in an imperfect ability to listen, think, speak, read, write, or to do mathematical calculations. The term includes such conditions as perceptual handicaps, brain injury, minimal brain dysfunction, dyslexia, and developmental aphasia. The term does not include children who have learning problems which are primarily the result of visual, hearing, or motor handicaps, of mental retardation, of emotional disturbance, or of environmental, cultural or economic disadvantage. A child who exhibits a discrepancy of 50 percent or more between expected achievement based on his intellectual ability and actual achievement, determined on an individual basis, shall be deemed to have a severe learning disability.[1]

A *hyperactive child*, in addition to having learning disabilities, is characterized by compulsive behavior, poor attention span, and an inability to sit still. A hyperactive child is not simply a very active youngster but one who simply can't stop moving, talking, making noise. He may also have sleeping problems and be bad-tempered.

The mother of one eight-year-old hyperactive kept a diary of what it is like living with her son:

An Ordinary Day in the Life of Hurricane Hal

7:15 . . . Alarm rings. He gets up, crosses room, turns it off, and goes back to bed. I wake him firmly but fairly gently at 7:30. I go back to kitchen to make his breakfast and fix his lunch. He goes back to sleep.

7:45 . . . I speak roughly, and he drags himself out of bed, goes to take shower, leaves towel on floor, shower dripping, lights on in bathroom, floor wet, pajamas where they fell, drawers all open, clean clothes on floor, radio and room lights on and staggers half-dressed to kitchen.

Can't find shoes, shoes are wet, shoes are muddy, shoes too small, lunch not right, sausage too cold, starving!, coffee too hot, coffee too cold, too much butter on toast, not enough butter on toast. Eats half a sausage, no toast, sips coffee. Can't find books, teases dog, says will feed dog when comes home, makes loud cat noises, needs money for overdue library book. I get money, he can't find library book, drops money on floor, won't pick it up, says doesn't care, has to be pushed into brushing hair (school regulation).

8:10 . . . Car pool honks, child grabs books, exits, leaving door open. I collapse and cry a little. Get up, clean house.

3:25 . . . Child returns. Bangs through door, tosses books on floor, gives me a quick hug, says "I love you," grabs banana, says "Why do we always have oatmeal cookies, why don't we ever have oatmeal cookies," says teacher was mean to him, fussed because he didn't have homework today, gets on bicycle, and goes off into neighborhood, back in a couple hours, "See ya, Mom."

3:46 . . . I look out window. See two little heads sneak past. The heads go toward tree house in our backyard. I quietly follow. Fireballs (wadded-up paper) begin to fly down from tree house. I go into tree house, find matches, paper, and stolen cigarettes. I send neighbor child home. I talk calmly, fingernails cutting into palms, about danger of fire to his person and to tree house and grounds. He says, "I just can't help it." Or "I didn't do it. Beth did it." Or "They were already burning when we got here, and we were just trying to put the fireballs out." I send him to room for an hour. Screams and yells and throws things. Kicks woodwork, pulls all clothes out of drawers, tears at screen at window, climbs to top shelf of closet and throws

toys down, tosses whole barrel of Lincoln Logs around
room.

5:00 . . . Hour is up, can't leave room until things are
straight again. Stuffs toys under bed, wads clothes into
drawers, leaves room. Storms around kitchen, starving!,
picks on sister, takes her book, bangs doors, pots, pans,
teases cat, starving! I do not have dinner ready yet. Am
climbing wall. Say "Go outside for a few minutes, but
don't leave the property." Child gets on bicycle, goes to
greenhouse next door, cons Coke, goes to bathroom, lights
fire in wastebasket with matches he found on greenhouse
office desk, woman employee throws water on fire, child
kicks her, leaves.

6:15 . . . Re-enters house, starving! I put his dinner on
table. Ignores knife, fork, and napkin, eats with fingers in
about thirty seconds. If he likes meal, he will eat. If not,
he will stalk to disposal and dispose of meal. Wants des-
sert. Eats that. Leaves floor full of crumbs, plate on table,
wants to watch television.

7:00 . . . Now the difficult part begins. Teacher has
asked me to spend fifteen minutes each evening to supervise his homework. Can't find assignment sheet, can't do
homework. Bangs door, slumps in chair, snaps point of
pencil, jumps on furniture, writes illegibly, says "Dam-
mit," won't add, scratches on paper, says "I'm too dumb,"
shows me scab picked off in school today, wants to talk
about fire truck he saw today, has to have immediate attention to athlete's foot, must show bump on knee, constant wiggles, loud noises, cracks knuckles, jiggles chair. I
give up. Fix martini.

7:28 . . . Storms, falls, bangs, runs through house.
Loud noises, teases dog, barks like one, starving!, in and
out of parents' room with minor crises after having been
told one thousand times that seven to nine o'clock is to be

spent in his room quietly. Starving! Must have ice cream, must have glass of wine. "Can I have a Coke?"

8:10 . . . Teacher calls. Says child is sweet and cheerful as long as she does not make any demands on him. Disrupting classroom. Sticking pins in other children. She loves him, he will run any errand, do any chore except concentrate on his work and own business. She's puzzled. Taking instruction on her day off at behavior modification school he attended last semester in order to learn how to cope with him. We discuss ratio of that school (3 to 1 versus 19 to 1 in St. George's) and how hard it is for her to give him all the attention he requires. Impossible situation. I fix another martini. And a double for his father.

9:00 . . . We scream and yell at him (or talk quietly, depending on endurance span) to go to his room and let us have our right of being and talking together. He goes. Very noisy in room, very messy getting into pajamas, plays a little.

9:18 . . . Sneaks out of room. Goes into kitchen. Climbs pantry shelves, opens and slams refrigerator door four or five times. Romps loudly and frantically with dog. Puts Pepsi bottle down disposal, which makes hideous noise. Father goes in and takes him by the scruff of the neck to his room. Turns on closet light (only one he has, all lamps are broken), and tells him not to get out of bed again.

9:42 . . . After a good deal of loud singing, yelling, and crashing, he is quiet. His father and I can't bear to utter a word; the silence is too golden. Everyone is tense, exhausted, emotional.

10:30 . . . House is dark. Parents sob, clutch, brace for another day. And the next day will be the same as the day before. Except for weekends. They're worse.

In the classroom a hyperactive child is the bane of the teacher's existence. He can't sit still at his desk, is con-

6 WHAT YOU CAN DOWHAT YOU CAN DO

stantly up and down, teases the other children, has to go to the bathroom, can't find his paper, wants to eat lunch now. He is a pest to his peers and often seeks the companionship of younger children over whom he has some power. He also finds learning difficult and frustrating.

The result is that the hyperactive child has to be placed in a special class or school that may not prove to be of much help until the *cause* of his hyperactivity can be diagnosed and treated. The same may be said of the learning disabled child who doesn't suffer from hyperactivity. His progress will be difficult and limited until the source of the problem can be identified and treated.

Fortunately Hal's parents eventually found help through a proper diagnosis and treatment of his problems, but it wasn't easy. It took several years to find answers before their son was restored to a normal, achieving, and successful life.

Why?

The answer lies in the fact that it is only in recent years that much attention has been paid to hyperactivity by the medical profession, and then unfortunately primary attention was focused on the use of drugs as an answer.

Historically there are reference points going back to the last century that give evidence of the phenomenon of hyperactivity. A nineteenth-century German physician, Heinrich Hoffmann, described the hyperactive child in a bit of verse entitled "Die Geschichte von Bappel-Philipp," which translates to "The Story of Fidgety Phil."

> Fidgety Phil
> He won't sit still
> He wriggles
> And giggles . . .
> And when scolded by his parents,
> The naughty restless child
> Grows still more rude and wild.

What the incidence of hyperactivity among children in the nineteenth century was, we have no idea, but since World War II in the United States it is estimated to be 5 to 10 per cent[2] of elementary schoolchildren. The syndrome may be on the increase, but that has not been established at the present time.

The *hyperkinetic behavior syndrome,* or, as we shall refer to it, *hyperactivity,* describes a complex group of problems occurring primarily in children and manifesting itself in a way disturbing to families, teachers, and the children themselves. This kind of disturbance, also called *MBD* (minimal brain dysfunction),[3] has no single cause or simple answer. The major symptoms we see are an increase of purposeless physical activity and a significantly impaired attention span. This inability to control physical motion can cause havoc in the home, at play with peers, and in the classroom.

Hyperactivity is a matter *not* simply of degree of activity but of quality or type of physical motion. The activity appears driven, compulsive. The child is easily distracted, jumping from one idea or interest to another with little or no focused attention. The core symptom that has emerged from medical research and commentary is *attention deficit,* or extreme shortness of attention span.

DIAGNOSIS OF HYPERACTIVITY

It is important to understand that hyperactive behavior may accompany other illnesses or in some cases may have relatively simple causes. Some perfectly healthy children may have difficulty maintaining attention because of *stress* in school or at home. A child may be inattentive and restless because of hunger, poor teaching, overcrowded classrooms, or lack of understanding. The important point here is not to confuse true hyperactivity with such behavior or with the normal superabundance of childhood energy.

Clinically, hyperactive children are defined as those whose intelligence ranges from low normal to high. The vast majority of children with this syndrome have specific learning disabilities.

In order to make an adequate evaluation of the hyperactive and learning disabled child, the following data is necessary:

1. Prenatal, perinatal, and postnatal history
2. Family medical history
3. Medical examination
4. Neurological and functional examination
5. Basic blood chemistries, including a five-hour glucose tolerance test

Clinical experience reveals that most hyperactive–learning disabled children have multiple problems that are causing their difficulties. These usually have a combination of biochemical, metabolic, nutritional, or allergy problems along with motor and perceptual difficulties. Consequently treatment usually requires a combination of therapies. These will be discussed in detail in subsequent chapters.

NOTES

[1] Federal Law PL 94-142, Part 200.1.

[2] P. Wender, *Minimal Brain Dysfunction in Children* (New York: John Wiley & Sons, 1976), p. 62.

[3] S. Clemens, *Minimal Brain Dysfunction in Children,* Monograph no. 3 (Washington, D.C.: U. S. Public Health Service, 1966).

II

What's a Parent to Do?

Parents of hyperactive children often find themselves frustrated in trying to find help for their child. In the past physicians often advised parents not to worry, that the child would grow out of the problem. (Some parents still hear this philosophy.) In more recent years stimulant drugs have been introduced as an answer to the hyperactivity syndrome. A review of the medical literature reveals that more research has been done on drug therapy than on any other mode of treatment. Today, unfortunately, it is the most widely favored approach to hyperactivity, despite the known dangers and harmful side effects of a drug such as Ritalin. Perhaps parents don't read the warnings listed in the "Contraindications" section of the product-information leaflet that the drug manufacturer provides, as required by federal law.

"Ritalin should not be used in children under six years, since safety and efficacy in this age group have not been established," cautions the leaflet. There is more:

Sufficient data on safety and efficacy of long-term use of Ritalin in children with minimal brain dysfunction are not yet available. Although a causal relationship has not been established, suppression of growth (i.e., weight gain and/or height) has been reported with the long-term use of stimulants in children. . . . There is some clinical evidence that Ritalin may lower the convulsive threshold in patients with prior history of seizures, and, very rarely, in absence of history of seizures and no prior EEG evidence of seizures.

The leaflet also contains an "Adverse Reactions" list:

Nervousness and insomnia are the most common adverse reactions but are usually controlled by reducing dosage and omitting the drug in the afternoon or evening. Other reactions include hypersensitivity (including skin rash, urticaria, fever, arthralgia, exfoliative dermatitis, erythema multiforme with histopathological findings of necrotizing vasculitis, and thrombocytopenic purpura); anorexia; nausea; drowsiness; blood pressure and pulse changes, both up and down; tachycardia; angina; cardiac arrhythmia; abdominal pain; weight loss during prolonged therapy. Toxic psychosis has been reported. Although a definite causal relationship has not been established, the following have been reported in patients taking the drug: leukopenia and/or anemia; a few instances of scalp hair loss. In children, loss of appetite, abdominal pain, weight loss during prolonged therapy, insomnia, and tachycardia may occur more frequently; however, any of the other adverse reactions listed may also occur.

Sydney Walker III, M.D., director of the Southern California Neuropsychiatric Institute and consultant to the New York Institute for Child Development, who has worked with hyperactive children, criticizes the careless and widespread use of these drugs. At the institute's 1976 conference, he indicated that the danger of using amphetamines for hyperactivity "is the threat of masking the symptoms of other possible disease processes. It is not logical or prudent to write a prescription for amphetamines before a careful, detailed sorting out of histories, detailed physical examinations and appropriate biochemical and neurophysiological assessments have been done."

Dr. Walker points out that it does not make sense to use a drug that might get results without knowing why and that such use involves the risk of masking of symptoms that emanate from an undiagnosed cause. He has warned that Ritalin is dangerous and inappropriate and can have a damaging effect on the brain in some instances. Ritalin can cause disruption of the growth hormone, can produce deleterious effects, and is not curative. It actually prevents a proper diagnosis from being made.

Dr. Walker places part of the blame for the overuse of drugs in treating hyperactive children on the drug industry and its "high-pressure Madison Avenue sales pitches." He says, "Drug companies often misrepresent their products and encourage the use of large amounts of drugs at the expense of the nation's health." Particularly with hyperactive children, according to Dr. Walker, drugs are being used as an "expedient and the result is that medication often masks the true problem. Drugs delay the diagnosis and superimpose the sense of well-being, which is not realistic." Dr. Walker would like to see a "thorough overhaul" of the existing Food and Drug Administration requirements relating to the testing of new drugs before they are placed on the market. This would mean "more stringent requirements in terms of experimentation, proper studies, double-blind testing, controls, and pharmaceutical evaluation to determine efficacy." And that means a good deal more than the list of adverse reactions that manufacturers report.

The key point of Dr. Walker's remarks is that the "fast and easy" treatment for learning and behavior disorders can be dangerous. A differential diagnosis that explores a variety of possible causes is extremely important if valid and effective treatment is to be prescribed.

However, the parents' problem is complicated. There is
the pressure of living with the hyperactive child. There is
further pressure from the school; some parents have been
threatened with expulsion of their hyperactive child from
school if he is not put on medication to slow him down.

In a research study, "Legal Aspects of Drugging the
Hyperactive Child," Joseph Fleming of the New York
University Law Clinic reports that the real reason for
drug therapy is apparently not a burning desire to cure
the child but merely a need to stop the unpleasant symptoms. "It is a fact," says Fleming, "that most referrals to
doctors and clinics for drug treatment are through the
school system. These referrals are accepted by doctors
with alarmingly little concern for whether the symptom,
hyperactivity, is an indication of some other problem such
as carbon monoxide toxicity, infestation with parasites,
metabolic disorders, heart problems or any one of a host
of others."[1] In other words, the symptoms are attacked
and eradicated through continued drug therapy, but the
underlying problem goes unchecked, posing a potential
danger to the health and safety of the child.

Perhaps one of the most telling arguments against the
use of Ritalin or other stimulant drugs is that recent research indicates that it does not really help a child's learning process. In fact, in light of studies that independent
researchers have conducted, one could say a well-
behaved child was a poor alternative. Among these researchers are Herbert E. Rie, Ph.D., Ellen D. Rie, Ph.D.,
and Sandra Stewart, M.D., all of the Department of Pe-
diatrics at Ohio State University, and J. Philip Ambuel,
M.D., of Children's Memorial Hospital in Chicago. Re-
porting in the *American Journal of Orthopsychiatry*,[2] the
Rie group found that although Ritalin did quell the antisocial behavior of the children, as advertised, it did not
in any general sense "improve their learning ability." The

skills that did improve were peripheral to the learning process. The areas of improvement were so minor and the improvements themselves so inconsistent that the changes seem irrelevant.

"These findings," the group reported, "confirm our previous conclusion that Ritalin is not a suitable 'treatment' for problems of learning." You can't improve a child's scholastic performance by eliminating his antisocial behavior, these researchers concluded. They believe this issue to be critical because they have found that "behavioral changes, including changes in moment-to-moment classroom performance, are incorrectly perceived by teachers as positive changes in *achievement*." When this misunderstanding occurs, "there may be no further effort to enhance the child's learning, for there appears to be no reason to try. In this sense, the drug effects may obscure the learning problems and increase the probability of their being ignored."

The Rie group concluded that Ritalin should be used "far more sparingly and critically than has been the case in the past several years." They emphasized that the unaffected functions clearly require different treatment altogether. But they felt it is also possible that other kinds of treatment "may be more difficult during periods of drug treatment." The Rie group concluded that, at best, drugs provide a way of reaching children who may appear unreachable. Once some sort of communication between the child and his parents and others is established, drug treatment should give way to other methods of dealing with the child's problems. Sole reliance on the drug and uncritical acceptance of "positive evaluations of the effects by parents and teachers should be avoided," the research team emphasized, "at all costs."

Another alternative that has been used with hyperactive children is behavior modification. This technique is based on a system of correcting or changing behaviors by rewarding good behavior and punishing bad behavior. The rewards might be as simple as a few words of praise; the punishment, words of criticism. Candy and other foods are often used as rewards. This method can be effective with many children if it is properly structured by capable practitioners, but it will not have any lasting effect on a truly hyperactive child, who cannot control his compulsive behavior. Also, giving candy to a hyperactive child who has low blood sugar may simply increase aberrant behavior.

Many hyperactive children have been treated by psychotherapy. This may have some salutary effect on the child because he may develop emotional or psychological problems as a consequence of the fact that he is a school failure and can't get along with his peers. Again, however, psychotherapy by itself will have little value if the causes of the hyperactivity are not diagnosed and treated.

New hope was raised recently with the publication of Dr. Ben Feingold's book *Why Your Child Is Hyperactive*.[3] Dr. Feingold developed a diet for hyperactive children who seemed to be allergic or sensitive to some additives. Research on the Feingold diet, sponsored by the federal government, has not been conclusive but indicates the need for further study. Research conducted by the New York Institute for Child Development combined with clinical experience with hundreds of hyperactive children supports the Feingold theory in part but indicates that the more significant factor in these children is their reaction to sugar because of a difficulty in metabolizing carbohydrates (see Chapter 6 for details). The most valuable result of Dr. Feingold's work has been to bring attention to the fact that food sensitivities and allergies are important factors in evaluating and treating hyperactivity. It may well be that the Feingold diet did not hold up successfully in research because sugar was not eliminated along with additives and preservatives.

What, then, is a parent to do who has a hyperactive child? We've pointed out some of the don'ts or at least indicated the ineffectiveness of drugs, psychotherapy, and behavior modification in dealing with hyperactivity and learning disabilities. What the parent must do is to understand the nature of the problem and seek competent medical diagnosis and a program of treatment.

The New York Institute for Child Development has developed an effective evaluation and treatment program for hyperactive and learning disabled children. The remaining chapters of this book explain the basis and nature of this clinical approach in order to help the parent understand the scope of the problem and know what to do to help his or her child.

NOTES

[1] New York Institute for Child Development Conference, 1976.
[2] Herbert E. Rie and Ellen D. Rie, "Effects of Ritalin on Underachieving Children: A Replication," *American Journal of Orthopsychiatry* 46, no. 2 (April 1976).
[3] Ben Feingold, *Why Your Child Is Hyperactive* (New York: Random House, 1974).

III

The Process of Child Development

To properly understand the nature of learning disabilities and hyperactivity, it is important to understand the normal process of child development. This will enable us to see more clearly what can and does go wrong, when a child is not functioning up to the norm, and how this affects learning.

There are probably no two accomplishments in an individual's existence that are more eagerly awaited or more proudly acclaimed than an infant's first steps and first words. Even the diploma received on graduation day, after the young person has successfully coped with many years of instruction and tests, is scarcely rewarded with the same spontaneous joy. Strangely enough the ease with which the individual mastered the academic skills that lead to graduation day was probably closely related to the appropriate timing of the development of just such skills as walking and talking. But although parents intuitively recognize the ability to walk as a milestone, they are probably unaware of the intricate pattern of growth that precedes this attainment.

From birth to eight years of age, there is a predicted pattern of growth called *functional growth,* just as there is an expected pattern of physical growth. This functional growth is evidenced by the ability of the central nervous system to interpret increasingly sophisticated stimuli received through the five senses and to react in an increasingly sophisticated and specialized manner. Functional growth, then, means the development of the ability to receive and respond to sensory information that enables the child to feel, move, gain a sense of his own body in space, and eventually to read, understand, and speak as well as to perform manual and mental tasks.

The sense of touch is the key to this. Its development begins in the uterus and continues throughout early childhood. An infant first becomes aware of pain and pressure at about two weeks after birth. Light touch and temperature changes usually become meaningful around two to three months of age. After this, body awareness begins to develop. Through random movements the baby is made aware of his body parts, and he makes his first accidental attempts at locomotion. The child pushes against something and has the experience of "*Wow, I moved!*" What did he do? Soon he will try again.

Fairly quickly he associates a kick with movements of his body. Then one day he pushes with his hand and turns over. So he tries that again, too. These are the first steps in the development of purposeful movement. This is the beginning of a predetermined pattern of growth through which, within approximately six years, the child progresses from a level of functioning that is merely reflexive to a youngster with the skills necessary for reading and writing and riding a tricycle. None of these skills develop in a vacuum. They are the result of stimulation received and interpreted by the central nervous system.

How does this happen?

Think of the brain as a computer. This is a simplification, but it is useful in understanding how all this works. We have inputs (the five senses, which are the *only* route to the brain), and we have outputs (moving, talking, and so on). The process of wiring the computer and programming data banks and outputs is fourfold: myelinization, proliferation, the processing of external stimulation, and the storing and retrieving of information. These processes occur simultaneously.

What is *myelinization?* At birth a nerve has a thin sheath surrounding it called *myelin.* This sheath serves to carry nutrients to the nerve and waste products away

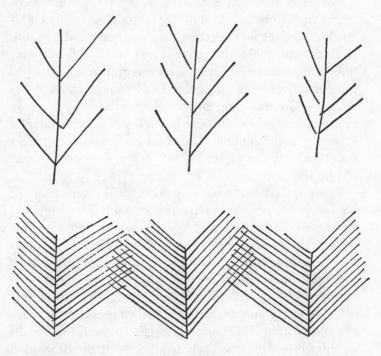

(These drawings are schematic, but actual photographs have been taken.)

from it, as well as to protect impulses and channel their direction through the nervous system. As a nerve is used and stimulated, the sheath around it thickens (the process of myelinization), and the nerve itself grows in diameter. As in electricity, the more current you need to run through a wire, the heavier the wire must be, and the thicker the insulation around it needs to be. Myelinization develops automatically through use. But if a nerve is not used, myelinization does not occur, or it may be insufficient. This process is evident in any nerve and in the spinal cord and brain.

As nerves are being myelinated, they are also *proliferating*. Within the brain is a network of nerve structures that start out very simply, like the root of a plant that gradually develops tiny tendrils as it grows. As the nerves are called upon to function and sensory information is being taken in, they thicken and elongate, and the branches proliferate until it becomes an intertwining forest.

This intertwining occurs through *use*. If these nerve cells are unused, the thickening and growth patterns do not develop. To be used, impulses must travel into the system on sensory nerve pathways. The easiest demonstration of how this occurs is by the *reflex arc*. The reflex arc is a way of describing what happens when the body receives information through one of the senses. Actually, two things happen almost instantaneously: (1) The bodily part affected reacts to the sensory stimulation, and (2) information about what has happened is transmitted to the brain, so that the brain is aware of whatever stimulation has occurred.

For example, if you are tapped on the knee with a reflex hammer, an impulse is transmitted to the spinal cord and immediately back to the point of sensation, so that the knee *jerks*. But at the same time a message is sent to the brain to make you aware that your knee has been tapped. The same process takes place whenever any of the sense organs, the eyes, the ears, the nose, and so on, receives stimulation.

Here is what this arc reflex process looks like:

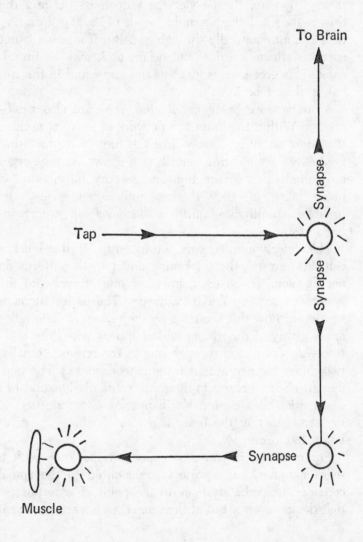

The initial impulse must be strong enough to travel its path so as to get a reaction. It also must be strong enough to jump the synapse (space between nerve endings) to travel to your brain in order for you to know what occurred at your knee. To some degree this happens with every sensation or impulse your five senses receive. This is the way information (sight, sound, touch, taste, and smell) gets to your brain: from impulses coming in by way of the five senses and traveling along nerve fibers to the area of the brain that is concerned with each.

Once the information reaches the brain, it is stored in molecules, the filing system for information and knowledge. These molecules also transmit information into and out of the brain on chains, each responsible for a piece of information. This system works something like this:

A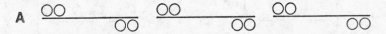

This is a free chain ready to accept information. Johnny tries to put his finger in a light socket, and Mommy yells, "No! No!" Mommy's urgent message moves on an impulse to the information channels in the brain. These channels become the means by which the developing brain is programmed for consistent responses to outside stimuli.

B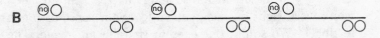

Then Johnny pulls the pots out of the cupboard, and Mommy again yells, "No! No!" Again the brain is being programmed to respond.

C

The process continues until the whole chain is programmed for yes and no (and/or for colors, touches, and other sensory information).

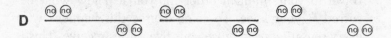

When the chain is complete, information is easily retrieved and is transmitted almost instantly.

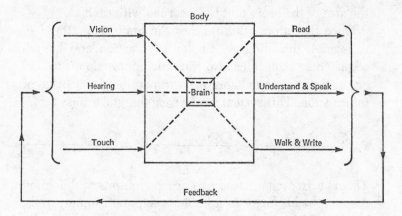

There is, in addition, a feedback system. This is a self-monitoring mechanism of the brain and body that tells input how output is doing. For example, the hard-of-hearing man shouts because he has lost his auditory feedback. The leg you've sat on for so long that it went to sleep won't work right because you've lost your sense of touch feedback. We squint our eyes to sharpen an image. The feedback system then becomes a corrective system through which the brain adjusts the sensory and body motor information as it is received in order to function properly. When you're getting ready to write, you know where your arm, hand, and fingers are and how to move them to complete the task and make the letters of your name.

Now let's go back to the computer analogy and put these processes together. All four processes of the central nervous system develop simultaneously. By the time the child is eight years of age, all systems (i.e., myeliniza- tion, proliferation, processing of sensory stimulation, and storage and retrieval of information) should be com- pletely developed and functioning. When all systems are properly developed, the child should be capable of learn- ing, speaking, reading, writing, computating, and execut- ing sophisticated movements of the body such as those required for ball sports and bike riding.

But this is only the internal, physical growth of the cen- tral nervous system. Next we will look at the external process of human development, as observed and catego- rized by physicians and clinicians, which occurs simulta- neously with the development of the brain and nervous system. For our purposes we will call it the *four stages of development*.

The Four Stages of Development

Neurological organization is the ability of the brain to take in all information, process it, organize it, and direct the proper response. To achieve optimum neurological or- ganization and finally to learn properly, a child must pass through and master a series of developmental stages. Al- though a stage *may* be missed without resulting in an ob- vious inadequacy, the chances are strong that the mature individual will be less efficient in some areas. Thus, it is possible that a hyperactive or learning disabled child lacks complete neurological organization. Obviously if a child is grossly injured, full normal development may be limited. In the case of hyperactive and learning disabled children the problem is more subtle and less severe. For example, if an infant is hospitalized for an extended period or confined to a playpen for too much time without sufficient stimulation, normal development may be affected. As we go through the stages of development, you will be able to see this more clearly.

Let's look at the normal processes of development that lead to neurological organization. The development of a child from birth to age six can be characterized by the types of mobility that are present in the four progressive developmental stages. Although the stages of mobility are of obvious importance in that they allow the child to learn to walk, many vital visual, manual, and auditory skills are being refined as the child explores his environment, first on his tummy, then on his hands and knees, and finally on his feet, walking upright. This is the time when the visual skills necessary for reading are being developed and when the auditory discrimination needed for phonetics and spelling is in formation.

At birth the infant reacts to his environment in a reflexive manner. There is not true mobility, but the arms and legs move in a general manner. Vision is observed as the pupils of the eyes constrict when stimulated by light. And although Daddy is very proud of his son's strength as the baby holds on so tightly to his fingers that he can lift the child up, the fact is, this grasp *is* a reflex; the infant cannot let go. Manual function is limited to the grasp reflex. This stage lasts until the infant is about two and a half months old.

The next stage is characterized by alternate one-sided function. For example, the child looks at the rattle in his right hand with his right eye. In turning from one side to the other, the infant may have rolled over, but up until now there has been no real forward movement. At this stage the infant starts to crawl as a form of mobility. This involves moving forward with his abdomen on the floor, pulling with his arms and pushing with his legs. As he experiments with various movements, he eventually finds that the most efficient way to move is to pull with one hand and push with the corresponding leg. Then he alternates and uses the other side of his body. As he moves along in this fashion, he is following his hand visually with one eye while the other eye's vision is blocked by the floor. This is the beginning of the development of eye-hand skill, and he is also able to control his hand enough so that he can let go of objects. The infant at this stage rarely uses both sides of his body in unison. That comes with the third stage, which starts at around eight months.

The third stage of development is a *bilateral* stage, which means the child starts using both sides of his body together for a more efficient form of locomotion, creeping on all fours. This involves moving forward on hands and knees, using the left hand and right leg simultaneously, then the right hand and left leg. He is ready to explore his environment—coffee tables, light plugs, kitchen cabinets. Now there is real evidence of goal-directed behavior in the child's movements.

The visual stimulation that occurs at this time is vital for the development of *binocular vision* (the coordinated use of both eyes). As the infant moves across the floor, he watches his hands, both eyes focusing first on one hand and then on the other. The infant still grasps things in his fists, but as he puts his hands down on the floor and manipulates the many things he finds, he is starting to develop the function necessary for cortical opposition. *Cortical opposition* (the ability to touch the tips of thumbs and forefingers together) is the skill that allows the child to hold a pencil correctly, tie his shoe, or button his clothes.

In the fourth stage the infant becomes a *walker*. At first he is unsteady and must raise his arms to facilitate balance; finally with continued practice he will develop a cross-pattern walk (right hand swings forward as left leg goes forward). This stage starts on the average around age sixteen months and runs until about age forty-six months. This is a long stage, but the functions that are now being refined are those that are distinctly human. Together with walking, speech should progress from couplets to the ability to communicate in short sentences. Cortical opposition, so necessary for correct pencil grasp, is developing at this time. The child starts moving into the world of the third dimension and acquires a perception of depth. The development of this *visual skill* in conjunction with improved walking becomes evident as the child does something seemingly as simple as walking down steps correctly. Initially the child will walk two steps, then get down on his hands and knees and creep down them backward; then he will master one step at a time. This is demonstrated in that agonizingly slow progress down a flight of steps when Mother has one arm overloaded with laundry and has firm hold of her child's hand with her other hand and the child solidly plants both feet on each step before proceeding to the next one.

The fourth stage is characterized by the emergence of one side of the body as preferred for skilled tasks. This is most obvious in the development of handedness. It is not only in the area of manual function that a skilled side is developed; the child will also develop a preferred foot and eye for skills. Obvious indications of the preferred eye would be the one chosen when using a telescope or a camera. The foot chosen for kicking or hopping would be the skilled foot.

The outside limit for the normal attainment of laterality (i.e., left- or right-handedness) is around eight years of age, but most children seem to resolve their laterality between five and seven years of age. It seems that ideally the skill attainment would be one-sided; in other words, the child would be right-handed, right-footed, and right-eyed. However, a great deal of controversy rages over the necessity for the preferred hand and preferred eye to be established on the same side, or unilaterally. We will discuss some aspects of this issue in Chapters 4 and 5.

Although we have just described development in terms of four identifiable stages, it must be remembered that development is an ongoing process, with mobility setting the groundwork for visual and manual development. As the body and brain respond to stimulation, the developmental process is reinforced, and the nervous system grows and becomes more efficient. It has been said that movement is the key to all learning. As each new skill is acquired and perfected, it becomes the foundation for moving on to the next skill. Many children move through these years of development following the prescribed sequence. Some children, however, skip stages or slip too quickly through a stage. For example, some learning disabled children will have skipped a stage of development and will have started walking before they have developed through a bilateral creeping stage. This leads to loss of binocularity (two-eyedness), which reduces visual attention span because both eyes are not working together.

As we will explain more fully in Chapters 4 and 5, the diagnosis of a learning disabled or hyperactive child involves testing the functioning of that child for performance in the stages of development in order to determine what stage may have been missed or not sufficiently matured.

CAUSES OF DEVELOPMENTAL PROBLEMS

There are three major factors that can affect the developmental progress and thus inhibit the process of neurological organization: genetic factors, traumatic factors, and environmental factors.

Genetic (or Inherited) Factors

We all inherit certain factors that influence our looks, our growth, and our development. Everyone knows about inheriting color of hair and eyes, but we also inherit tendencies toward some more subtle factors. These can include inborn errors of metabolism resulting in an inability to digest certain foods. This predisposition may affect the developing child's responses to his environment, such as early walking (skipping the bilateral stage), left-handedness, or ambidexterity. It is because of these factors that maximum environmental opportunities should be afforded the growing infant and child so that he can overcome these problems as he progresses through each stage.

Traumatic Factors

Potential dangers that can affect normal developmental progress can include any of a number of factors. None of these apply in *every* case. Many children have some of these factors in their histories and do not have problems; whereas many children with difficulties do not have these predictors. However, they do appear often enough in the histories of children with problems to bear some credence.

During the prenatal period (pregnancy) the mother's biochemical status affects her child. Her diet is crucial to the baby's development from a purely nutritional standpoint and, it is important to remember, because brain cells are being formed in the last six months of pregnancy (and the first three months of life) and must have the proper nutrients in sufficient quantity to allow full growth of the brain.

Any *drugs* taken by the expectant mother may affect

the unborn baby. Certainly imbalances (such as thyroid imbalance or hormone deficiency) must be corrected, but use of unnecessary medications or drugs should be avoided. Even aspirin is suspect! An extreme example of the consequences is the drug addict mother, who produces an addicted newborn. That is without question a hard way to begin life. Hormone usage is open to question. Birth control pills may alter proper balances we don't yet appreciate. Pregnancy-retention drugs may cause difficulties. We're not yet sure whether the drug causes problems or whether a defective fetus is being retained that, without interference, might have spontaneously aborted. One case in point would be a chromosome defect that would produce Down's syndrome (mongoloid) child.

Rh incompatibility has been, for the most part, conquered. When there is an Rh factor (positive blood type in the mother and negative blood type in the father), the baby will have Rh-negative blood type, which is incompatible with the mother's. The mother's natural defenses develop antibodies to protect her from a harmful reaction to the child's blood. However, she passes her antibodies on to the child. If those antibody levels are high enough (usually after two or three pregnancies), the baby will be "allergic" to his own blood. Hence, exchange transfusions have to be done to allow the baby to live healthily and then produce his own blood cells. Within recent years scientists have developed a substance called RhoGAM that can be injected into the mother after pregnancy to eradicate that particular antibody and begin a subsequent pregnancy as though it were her first.

The perinatal period (delivery and the first few weeks after birth) also holds potential dangers. Prematurity, of course, affects the ability of the baby to support his own life, depending on the maturity of his systems to breathe and collect oxygen from his lungs to pass to the rest of the body, to have sufficient red blood cells mature enough to carry oxygen, and to metabolize the other necessary vital elements. Difficult deliveries requiring forceps or other outside help, though necessary, pose potential problems because of trauma to the brain. Breech birth (rump delivered first), transverse position (baby sideways), or presentation feet first can all cause injury because of the need for manipulation of the fetus for proper headfirst delivery or because of the trauma caused by abnormal delivery. This can cause brain injury of greater or lesser degree.

Sometimes accidents happen that can interrupt the normal course of development. An infant who has to wear splints because of a hip problem will not have as much opportunity to practice his mobility. By the same token, a child who breaks a limb and is confined in a cast will have reduced efficiency for exploring his environment. A child who is having difficulty establishing handedness could well be influenced to make the wrong decision if one arm happens to be restricted by a cast at this crucial time.

Along with an opportunity for mobility, the developmental process is enhanced by auditory and visual stimuli. A child who is deprived of stimulation falls behind in his ability to perceive his environment and thus to learn appropriate responses. An infant does not just suddenly learn to say "mama" or "dada." He has been exercising his vocal cords with babbling for quite a while, but what produces "mama" or "dada" is the constant stimulation he has had from his hopeful parents, who have hopefully been saying it to him many times a day. It is through this constant stimulation that the infant modifies his own sounds to match what he hears. In the same manner a child cannot learn to discriminate visually between objects if he doesn't have an opportunity to see them.

A delayed birth cry (signaling breathing) should be cause for concern. A newborn must breathe as soon as he's out in the air. The umbilical cord collapses at birth, before it is cut, from the air pressure, and life support from the mother ceases, so he must begin breathing on his own. The adult brain can go only three minutes without oxygen before irreparable damage begins to occur; the newborn is even more susceptible to a lack of oxygen.

These birth traumas and difficulties are usually fairly simple to recognize. Dr. Virginia Apgar devised a rating system to evaluate newborns.

APGAR SYSTEM OF EVALUATING THE CONDITION OF THE NEWBORN

SIGN	SCORE		
	0	1	2
Heart-rate	Absent	Slow, below 100	Over 100
Respiratory rate	Absent	Slow, irregular	Good cry
Muscle tone	Limp	Flexion of arms or legs	Active motion
Reflex irritability*	No response	Grimace	Cough or silence
Color	All blue or all pale	Body pink, extremities blue	Completely pink

This method is used for evaluating the immediate postnatal adjustment of the newborn baby at one minute, five minutes, and ten minutes after birth. When the initial adjustment is good, the total score for the five signs is 8 to 10. Infants with lower scores require special attention. Scores under 4 indicate that the child's life-support systems are not functioning adequately.

* Tested by inserting the tip of a catheter into the nostril.

After the child has finally been successfully introduced to his new world, he is still vulnerable to potential perils. One of the first is inability to digest milk, resulting in colic. Many babies are allergic to milk, and it may take weeks to find a formula an allergic infant will thrive on. This is certainly important to his general welfare, because this period is also one during which numbers of brain cells are being formed and vital new sensations and experiences are beginning his developmental processes.

Environmental Factors

Much has been written about the obvious deprivation of stimulation that has occurred in many infant institutions (e.g., orphanages) and the resulting detrimental effect on the child's future performance. Even if a child has escaped trauma and the genetic code has been kind to him, he still needs a favorable environment if he is going to have the neurological organization necessary to realize his potential. Many of the effects of early trauma can be eased if a child is given a carefully chosen environment and plenty of opportunity to explore and use it.

Let's look at some of the elements for a good environment for a child's development. If, as a parent, you wanted to evaluate the adequacy of the environment for your own child, measure it against where the child is developmentally. The appropriate environment should be designed so that the child can reinforce the skills developed on the level at which he is functioning at the same time that there is the opportunity for him to move on to the next level. For example, for a child who is creeping, you would want to make the floor attractive to him in terms of space and objects so that he is motivated to move around and thus do a lot of creeping. At the same time you would want to provide opportunities for him to pull himself up into a standing position in preparation for the next stage, walking.

Many times environmental opportunities are curtailed unknowingly. An example of this would be too much confinement in a playpen. If the child is happy in the playpen, it would be an ideal placement while Mother gets her chores completed. However, a price may be paid for this early time-saver. If an infant spends large amounts of time in a playpen when he is in the creeping stage, he will probably miss much of the stimulation necessary at that level. The child obviously will not get in much creeping in such a confined area. He will probably pull himself up and maybe start walking before he is really ready. Thus, he will have missed an important opportunity for reinforcement of all the functions that are developed as a child creeps.

Factors that inhibit any of these sensations and experiences may interrupt the development of neurological organization. Playpens, more often used for the protection of the parent than for the protection of the child, restrict movement and exploration and can slow down sensorimotor development. Swaddling, casts (for hip problems), splints, and other such devices may be necessary for correction of physical difficulties, but parents should be aware of the opportunities denied the child and devise a substitute stimulation or, following the removal of the restrictive apparatus, make sure a stage of development has not been skipped. (This will be discussed in Chapters 4 and 5.)

Parents should also be sure adequate auditory, visual, and tactile stimuli are available to the developing child. If they know what functions should be developing at a given age, they can make sure as much opportunity as possible is supplied for each and all of the sensory modes and motor activities. They should also be sure to allow enough time for each stage to accomplish its task. To rush the child to the next level of development (e.g., from creeping to walking) may serve to create a gap in other areas, such as vision or manipulative skills.

Another way in which a child may be inhibited developmentally would be restrictive clothing. An infant must be free to move and explore. If his clothing interferes with this, he will not get the same stimulation as a child who is able to move freely.

Let's review the essential ideas presented in this chapter. In the process of a child's development there is a series of stages that he goes through from birth to eight years of age:

1. basic reflex stage (reaction to light and so on)
2. alternate one-sided stage
3. bilateral stage
4. walking stage

If any of these stages is skipped, it can cause problems in the development of the child's abilities to perform fine motor tasks such as reading and writing when he begins school.

Causes of developmental problems can be genetic (inherited), traumatic (birth injury), or environmental (extended confinement or lack of sufficient sensory stimulation).

It is important for parents to realize that they do not have to be physicians or neurologists in order to understand the basic processes of child development and to recognize when a child may not be functioning properly at a given age level. Professional diagnosis of problems may be necessary, but the parents usually are the primary witnesses to their child's development.

IV

Diagnosis: Seeking Causes

The first real tests of how well or efficiently a child has developed occur when the child moves into a new social experience, the world of other children, and of course when he enters school. At this juncture the child's behavior and performance are viewed critically. Some children have little or no problem. Some are slower to adjust. Others, though perfectly normal, have difficulty coping with the tasks they are asked to perform. Typically parents of hyperactive children are confronted with various problems in school by a teacher or other school official. Antisocial behavior, compulsive movement, lack of attention, and inability to perform normal school tasks are common occurrences cited. What can parents do?

The school may provide educational and psychological testing, but it seldom provides a search for *causes* in the child. Private diagnostic services and professionals that offer testing often fail as well. Parents faced with the task of having their child evaluated because of some inappropriate behavior may find the job much more difficult and frustrating than they had expected. Sometimes they end up with nothing more than involved descriptions of the child's behavior, all of which they knew already, but in much simpler terms.

The possible evaluations of a child's learning or behavioral problems can generally be put into two broad categories: those that look at *symptoms* and those that look for *causes*. Many educational and psychological evaluations identify areas in which a child's performance is depressed or below expected level. An example would be a child who is having trouble mastering reading. An evaluation might indicate that he has weak word-analysis skills. There is nothing more discouraging for parents than to pay a couple of hundred dollars to be told what they already knew. They knew the child couldn't read before the evaluation, and now they are told the child has a reading problem. On top of this the recommendation is tutoring for the skills he hasn't mastered.

What the parents haven't learned and what they need to know are the answers to basic questions: "What is the cause of my child's problem? It can't be the teacher. The other children know how to read. My child is bright enough, and he had the same instruction. Why didn't he learn?"

They feel he could learn if he just sat still long enough. The mother goes to the pediatrician, who slows him down with a drug. This treats the *symptoms* and allows the child to conform to the expected standards of behavior, but it does not answer the question "Why is he hyperactive?"

Or maybe the parents are told that the child is aggressive because he isn't successful in school. The recommendation is some type of counseling or therapy. This does not find the cause of his academic problems, and it would seem the best result they could hope for from such a course of treatment would be that their child would learn to be happy about being an underachiever.

These examples illustrate the category of evaluation that treats *symptoms*. Although some temporary changes may be seen as a result of these programs, they cannot provide long-term effectiveness. But if the cause of the problems can be determined and remediation can be aimed at the *cause*, then perhaps the reason for the problem can be removed and the child can move ahead and work up to his potential.

At the New York Institute for Child Development a careful and thorough evaluation process has been developed to pinpoint the *causes* of hyperactivity and learning disabilities. It is only with a complete diagnosis that proper treatment can be prescribed for these problems.

The checklists that follow were developed as a result of the New York Institute for Child Development's experience of seeing hundreds of children every year. They detail warning signals of physical conditions that may or may not be interfering with your child's achievement in academic and social areas.

If you answer yes to at least ten (or 20 per cent) of the questions, it may be that your child has a learning disability. This does not mean that your child is unintelligent. On the contrary, most children who suffer from learning disabilities have above-average intelligence.

PRESCHOOL

1. Is your child afraid of heights (e.g., won't climb on jungle gym, doesn't like to be picked up)?
2. Is your child extremely daring?
3. Is your child easily distractible?
4. Is your child always up and down from the table during meals?

5. Is your child a discipline problem?

6. Does your child seem to tune out at times?

7. Does your child frequently walk into things or trip?

8. Does your child find it necessary to touch everything he/she sees?

9. Is there inconsistency in your child's performance (i.e., one day he/she performs a task well; the next day he/she can't)?

10. Does your child have a short attention span?

11. Does your child get frequent headaches?

12. Is your child frustrated easily?

13. Does your child have difficulty keeping rhythm while dancing or clapping?

14. Is your child unusually sensitive to light, noise, touch, or certain clothing materials?

15. Was your child a late walker?

16. Was your child a prolonged tiptoe walker (i.e., one who walked on the tips of the toes)?

17. Was your child's speech late or abnormal?

18. Does your child have frequent nightmares?

19. Is your child a bed wetter?

20. Does your child have uncontrollable rage reactions?

21. Does your child complain of seeing things bigger or smaller than they are?

22. Is your child always tired?

23. Is your child unable to keep up with the other children's activity level?

24. Does your child have a poor appetite?

25. Does your child have a history of anemia of any type?

26. Is your child irritable before and/or shortly after meals?

27. Is your child easily fatigued?

28. Does your child exhibit excessive thirst?

29. Does your child crave sweets?

30. Has your child experienced excessive weight gain or loss?

31. Did your child have trouble learning to skip?

32. Does it seem that your child never pays attention to you?

33. Is your child unable to modulate his/her voice?

34. Does your child keep his/her head very close to the paper or tilt it back and forth when reading or writing?

35. Does your child have frequent stomachaches?

36. Does your child frequently go out of the lines when coloring?

37. Did your child have trouble learning how to tie and/or button and/or lace?

38. Does your child always seem to have a cold?

39. Was your child colicky?

40. Was your child an unusually cranky baby?

41. Was your child an unusually passive baby?

42. Does your child do everything to excess (e.g., laugh, cry, talk, sleep, perspire)?

43. Does your child have poor bowel or bladder control?

44. Does your child seem preoccupied with matches, fire, and so on?

45. Is your child a bully?

46. Is your child always picked on by his/her peers?

47. Is your child a loner?

48. Does your child's walking or running seem clumsy or disjointed?

49. Is your child ever purposely destructive?

50. Does your child have a history of allergies?

GRADES 1 TO 8

1. Does your child have difficulty understanding what he/she reads?

2. Does your child avoid ball sports or activities that involve catching and throwing a ball?

3. Is your child very afraid of heights (e.g., won't climb on the jungle gym, doesn't like to be picked up)?

4. Is your child extremely daring?

5. Does your child's running seem clumsy or disjointed?

6. Does your child get lost frequently?

7. Is your child easily distractible?

8. Does your child confuse right from left?

9. Does your child use one hand for some things and the other hand for other things?

10. Is your child always up and down from the table during meals?

11. Is your child a discipline problem?

12. Does your child go up or down stairs one step at a time?

13. Does your child seem very bright and articulate when in conversation but unable to understand what he/she reads?

14. Is your child the class clown?

15. Is your child not working up to his/her potential?

16. Does your child seem to tune out at times?

17. Is your child unusually forgetful?

18. Does your child find it necessary to touch everything he/she sees?

19. Does your child frequently walk into things or trip?

20. Is there inconsistency in your child's performance (i.e., one day he/she performs a task well; the next day he/she can't)?

21. Does your child have a short attention span?

22. Does your child move his/her lips while reading or follow the line with his/her finger?

23. Does your child get frequent headaches?

24. Is your child ever purposely destructive?

25. Is your child frustrated easily?

26. Is your child unusually sensitive to light, noise, touch, or certain clothing materials?

27. Was your child a late walker?

28. Was your child a prolonged tiptoe walker?

29. Was your child's speech late or abnormal?

30. Is your child a bed wetter?

31. Does your child have uncontrollable rage reactions?

32. Does your child complain of seeing things bigger or smaller than they are?

33. Is your child unable to keep up with the other children's activity level?

34. Does your child have a poor appetite?

35. Does your child have a history of allergies?

36. Is your child irritable before and/or shortly after meals?

37. Does your child crave sweets?

38. Has your child experienced excessive weight gain or loss?

39. Does your child frequently go out of the lines when coloring?

40. Did your child have trouble learning how to tie and/or button and/or lace?

41. Was your child colicky?

42. Was your child an unusually cranky baby?

43. Was your child an unusually passive baby?

44. Is your child a bully?

45. Is your child always picked on by his/her peers?

46. Is your child a loner?

47. Does your child seek out older or younger playmates?

48. Does your child's walking seem clumsy or disjointed?

49. When your child reads out loud, does he/she get mixed up or lose his/her place?

50. Does your child not complete his/her homework assignments?

HIGH SCHOOL

1. Does/did your child avoid sports or activities that involve catching and throwing a ball?

2. Does your child's walking or running seem clumsy or disjointed?

3. Is your child easily distractible?

4. Does your child confuse right from left?

5. Is/was your child always up and down from the table during meals?

6. Is your child a discipline problem?

7. Does your child seem very bright and articulate when in conversation but unable to understand what he/she reads?

8. Is your child the class clown?

9. Is your child below grade level or not working to his/her potential?

10. Is your child unusually forgetful?

11. Does your child frequently walk into things or trip?

12. Is there inconsistency in your child's performance (i.e., one day he/she performs a task well; the next day he/she can't)?

13. Does your child have a short attention span?

14. Does your child move his/her lips while reading or follow the lines with his/her finger?

15. Does your child get frequent headaches?

16. Is your child frustrated easily?

17. Does your child have difficulty keeping rhythm while dancing or clapping?

18. Was your child a late walker?

19. Was your child a prolonged tiptoe walker?

20. Was your child's speech late or abnormal?

21. Does your child complain that words blur or move on the page?

22. Is your child always tired?

23. Does your child have a poor appetite?

24. Does your child have a history of anemia of any type?

25. Is your child irritable before and/or shortly after meals?

26. Does your child exhibit excessive thirst?

27. Does your child crave sweets?

28. Has your child experienced excessive weight gain or loss?

29. Did your child have trouble learning how to tie and/or button and/or lace?

30. Was your child colicky?

31. Was your child an unusually cranky baby?

32. Does your child do everything to excess (e.g., laugh, cry, talk, sleep, perspire)?

33. Does/did your child have poor bowel or bladder control?

34. Is your child a bully?

35. Is your child always picked on by his/her peers?

36. Is your child a loner?

37. Does your child seek out younger or older playmates?

38. When your child reads out loud, does he/she get mixed up or lose his/her place?

39. Is your child ever purposely destructive?

40. Does your child complete his/her homework assignments on time?

41. Is your child often truant from school?

42. Does it seem your child never pays attention to you?

43. Is your child unable to modulate his/her voice?

44. Does your child keep his/her head very close to the paper or tilt it back and forth when reading or writing?

45. Does your child always seem to have a cold?

46. Does your child get frequent stomachaches?

47. Does your child seem to tune out at times?

48. Does your child have uncontrollable rage reactions?

49. Does your child have a history of allergies?

50. Was your child an unusually passive baby?

EVALUATION PROCESS

Once we suspect that a child is hyperactive or learning disabled, a full evaluation is called for. This evaluation must be done by professionals. At the New York Institute for Child Development, our evaluation includes the following tests:

Medical Tests

GTT	Five-hour glucose tolerance test
CBC	Complete blood count
SGPT	Tests liver function
SMA 12	Blood chemistry
Urin.	Urinalysis
T3, T4, T7	Tests thyroid function

Educational Tests

WRAT	Wide Range Achievement Test
Gray Oral	Oral Reading Paragraphs
Gates-MacGinitie	Silent Reading Achievement Tests
Roswell Chall	Tests word-analysis skills
Nolde-Muir	Lists of sight words, preschool to third grade levels
ABC Inventory	Determines kindergarten and school readiness
MRT	Metropolitan Readiness Tests

Functional Tests

Slosson	Measures verbal ability and arithmetic reasoning and computation.
K.I.	Kinesthetic integrity; measures ability to move body parts on touch, indicating integration of muscle systems.
Behavior Scale	Subjective estimate by parents of degree of child's activity in different situations.

Neurological Tests

Gross Motor	Tests coordination of major muscle groups and the ability of the child to perform activities.
Fine Motor	Tests coordination of small-muscle groups and the child's ability to accomplish fine skills.
Oculomotor	Evaluates smoothness of eye muscle coordination in all planes and the ability to converge.
Basic Motor	In testing developmental stages, indications of basic movement difficulties are obtained that explain higher-level problems and offer a basis for therapeutic programming.
Dominance	Handedness and footedness.

In addition, the following information is collected from the family: a full family medical history, a seven-day diet record of the child, and an activity scale of the child's behavioral patterns as evaluated by parents and teachers.

Educational testing provides information on where the child is having specific difficulties that indicate perceptual or auditory weaknesses. It also provides an objective basis against which changes in performance can be measured when the child is retested. Blood tests, family medical history, and diet analysis provide information about biochemical and nutritional problems that might interfere with the child's functioning. (These will be discussed in Chapter 6.)

One of the first concerns in evaluating a child should be a developmental and medical history that includes a prenatal, perinatal, and postnatal history and information on the appropriateness of the child's development of the basic skills (e.g., creeping, walking, and talking). This information can often give insights into the child's actual performance during the sensorimotor evaluation. A family medical history is important not only because it might give some information that would be relevant to the sensorimotor development of the child but also because it would give the nutritionist vital information on any evidence of diabetes and other disorders. It should include data about any medical problems the child had or has, any medication he has taken, and any allergy tendencies he might have had. Similar information on the parents can be of help in the interpretation of the child's problem.

Information from other professionals who have worked with the child should also be made available. Previous diagnoses and treatments can help complete the picture of the child's problem. A report from the teacher can help define the difficulties the child is having in the academic environment.

In evaluating a child with a view toward appropriate remediation, it must be remembered that the broader the picture that can be gained of the child, the more accurate the program that can be designed for the child. Therefore, not only a measure of current performance but also medical history factors that might contribute to his current disability are required; these factors can be signposts that corroborate a need for specific remediation techniques.

DEVELOPMENTAL EVALUATION

The evaluation of a child in terms of basic developmental functioning provides information on whether a child has developed basic functioning necessary to perform higher, fine motor skills such as reading, writing, and computation.

Development may be thought of as an inverted, carefully balanced pyramid. Each higher row of bricks represents a more complex level, involving more sophistication and more skills. The pyramid must be built from the bottom up, not from the top down, and must be carefully balanced.

```
\                                              /
 \   Function efficiently in the world        /
  \     Sophisticate all the skills          /
   \        Refine a skill                  /
    \        Gain a skill                  /
     \      Develop function              /
      \      Maintain life               /
       \        Reflex                   /
        \                               /
```

The building blocks must be complete and in balance in order for each progressive level to be added without the pyramid resembling the Leaning Tower of Pisa. That is, the pyramid must not have a precarious existence; it must be a bona fide building, able to stand on its own.

Therefore the relationship of each stage must be known in order to shore up the foundations and the level of skill building. The developmental evaluation is performed with the developmental scheme (as discussed in Chapter 3) in mind in order to assess each stage and its functions accurately. The quality of movement at each stage of development is the strongest indicator of improper functioning, and the tests used for each stage have been clinically shown to be related to anticipated functions in the world such as reading and writing. (See "Normal Development and Expected Performance" at the end of this chapter.) If a child fails at a particular stage, then we know where to begin a program of reinforcement therapy to stimulate that particular function.

Stage one, basic reflexes (e.g., knee jerk), should be tested, although we rarely find basic reflex abnormalities in the average hyperactive–learning disabled child. Another aspect that should be tested is the righting reflex (i.e., the ability to maintain an upright position, which begins with head control and sitting up in the infant). Inability to roll easily or in a straight line may indicate poor balance and spatial orientation because movement is related to the balance mechanisms that are necessary for a sense of one's self in space.

Stage two is the ability of a child to be unilateral, for example, to sight a rattle held in the right hand with his right eye or an object held in the left hand with his left eye. Evaluation of the second stage can give us definitive information relating to the child's mastery of future skills or eye-hand coordination.

The mobility of the unilateral level is crawling—the child lies on his stomach on the floor like a swimmer—and may be done homolaterally (arm and leg on the same side) or in cross pattern (arm and leg of opposite sides). In evaluating crawling, we are observing general performance as well as the specifics of the child's arm reaching far enough to give him effective pull, his leg bending far enough for him to get effective push, and his toe digging hard enough to give him maximum results from his leg push. We also observe the pulling arm as the body moves over it to be sure it rolls over with the palm up, which is the very beginning of good hand and finger function.

Vision at this level is tested on each side. The child covers one eye and follows a moving object with the other eye and points with the same hand. Each eye is evaluated in this manner. We make observations of the accuracy of both the hand and the eye in following the object: Does he move his eye, or does he prefer to move his head? Can he follow the object without stress? Are his movements jerky? Does he lose the object completely?

Correlations must be made between difficulties at a given level and expected functions at the skilled level. In other words, if a child is having difficulty at a school level —in reading or writing, for example—we go back down the developmental (skilled) levels to discover where there may be a developmental difficulty.

The third stage of development, the bilateral stage, seems to be closely related to efficient performance in many areas. At this stage the child is on all fours, that is, on his hands and knees. Also at this stage coordination of both sides of the body increases, and consequently there is continuing refinement of binocular vision and eye-hand coordination. The reason for this is that when the child is in a creeping position (i.e., on all fours), the eyes are learning to focus on hands and objects on the floor. Although good creeping per se is not a skill that is necessary for academic success, good binocularity and eye-hand coordination are necessary, and both these skills become functional as the child creeps. Thus, as the child creeps, he is laying the foundation for the skills required for reading and writing. A developmental evaluation of this stage should include creeping, eye-hand coordination, and fusion (the power of the brain to receive the two images from the two eyes and fuse them into one image).

An evaluation of creeping involves observing any aberrations that are present. Anyone who has ever observed an eight-month-old infant creeping rapidly across the floor cannot help but be amazed at the total coordination involved. He moves with the precision of a machine, left leg moving with right arm and right leg with left arm. He moves toward his goal in the perfect two-beat rhythm of a good trotter, his eyes guided by each hand as it moves forward. Although an older child, when he creeps, will not show the perfect synchronization of an infant's creep, certain basic elements should be present. The pattern should be a cross pattern, and the rhythm should be two-beat; in other words, opposite hand and knee should hit the floor at the same time. The toes should stay along the floor; they should not be lifted. The knees should move in a straight line. Many children who have binocularity problems will exhibit a narrow base in their knees (i.e., knees close together); sometimes this may be so obvious that the knees actually rub together as they move. The hand position is also a diagnostic indicator of poor organization at this level. The hands should be flat on the floor and should point straight ahead with the fingers close together. Many different hand positions are often seen. The most common aberration is the hands rotated out or up on fingers, so that the palms have no contact with the floor. These five aspects of creeping (pattern, rhythm, knee position, toe position, and hand position) are evaluated, and a general impression of the child's performance is recorded.

Another function that should be evaluated at this stage is eye-hand coordination. This can be done very simply by the parent or professional asking the child to follow a moving object with his finger. Sit in front of the child, about arm's length away, and have him point to your finger while you make a circle and a cross in the air. The size of your movements should be such that he can follow them with his eyes without moving his head. An evaluation is made of the child's ability to follow your finger with his own. The tester observes the eye movements. Do the child's eyes move smoothly and without stress, or are the movements jerky? Does he lose the object completely, or does he prefer to move his head rather than his eyes?

The two tests already discussed (creeping and eye-hand coordination) are easy to administer and do not require any equipment. However, in order to evaluate fusion, it is necessary to use some appropriate machines. Whatever machines are used, fusion should be evaluated at both far-point and near-point distances. In terms of function in the world this will evaluate the child's ability to fuse when looking at the blackboard and also when working on materials at his desk. Many youngsters will have adequate fusion at far point but will not have good fusion at near point (reading distance). Needless to say, if double vision exists at the reading distance, it can cause problems in learning to read and can reduce the amount of time the child is able to pay attention to work at near point. The child who works at a desk with his head way down close to the paper may well have fusion problems at the appropriate distance, so he moves in and rests his head on his elbow, blocking out one eye and thus clearing up the image.

If evaluations of a child at the bilateral stage indicate that he is disorganized at this level, he will show problems in specific functions at school and at home. Generally this child is poor in sports, particularly those involving a ball. This child is often disorganized in terms of himself and his belongings. His shirttail is always hanging out of his pants, and his papers are always hanging out of his notebook. Pencil grasp is poor, often using a thumb wrap instead of thumb-finger opposition. His handwriting is messy, and he has trouble organizing his material on a page. He is also the child who had difficulty learning to tie his shoes, to button buttons, and to zip zippers. Where reading is concerned, this is the child who may have great trouble using phonics. He may be able to learn the complicated rules, but he has difficulty hearing the sounds.

The children who have poor binocularity may well be labeled shy or lazy, when actually they are coping with their disability. The youngster with poor binocularity may rarely look someone in the eye, and he often walks with eyes downward. He's not shy; it's just that if he looks up, he sees double. This same child may do well in his work one day and then do poorly the next day. The assumption is that if he can do well one day, he could do well every day if he wanted to. The fact is that his performance may well be related to the state of his fusion and the energy he has on a given day to cope with the stress of working at near point.

In order to determine if poor organization at the bilateral stage is a factor in the child's inability to cope with the world, information from three areas must be evaluated. First, we would look at the child's developmental history: Did he creep? How did he creep? How long did he creep? Second, we would evaluate his creeping, binocularity, and eye-hand coordination. Third, we would identify his problems in functioning in the world: Can he catch a ball? Can he tie his shoes? Can he read? Can he write? With the information from these areas, we would then have a basis for making a decision about the child's need for treatment at the bilateral stage.

The fourth stage of functional development that must be evaluated is walking. This stage, along with the creeping stage, is closely related to efficient performance. Visually, the child's functioning is becoming increasingly sophisticated. There should now be skilled control of the eyes without the need for the hand to guide them, and there is also the development of stereoptic vision, or the ability to see the world in the third dimension. The developmental therapist would thus evaluate three areas: walking, oculomotor control, and stereopsis.

Walking is evaluated in two ways: the normal or functional walk, and a stylized cross-pattern walk. Normal efficient walking is in a cross pattern; that is, as the left foot moves forward, the right arm swings forward. The major clues to a poor functional walk are hands always in pockets and feet toeing in. Both of these make a cross-pattern walk difficult. If the hands are in the pockets, then the tendency is to move the right leg and right shoulder together at the same time. Cross-pattern walking is impossible if the hands are always in the pockets. The child who turns his toes in will also have trouble walking efficiently in a cross pattern because his balance will be threatened. Functional walking is evaluated as the child walks into the office or down the hall. If we specifically ask the child to walk for us, we may not see his normal pattern because he wonders what it is we want.

When demonstrating the cross-pattern walk, the therapist does so by actually pointing at his/her toes, that is, right index finger pointing at left toe, then left index finger pointing at right toe. The therapist then asks the child to walk in the same manner. The child is evaluated on his ability to maintain the cross pattern. Some cannot and are just as happy walking so that their left hand points to their left foot and their right hand to their right foot. Is the child's walking smooth and efficient? Or is his balance threatened, or do his legs get stiff, like a soldier's? These would be indications of disorganization at this level.

Oculomotor control at this stage is evaluated in two ways. First, the child's ability to follow a moving target smoothly and without stress is tested. During this procedure, the child's head should not move; rather, his eyes should do the work. Second, the child's ability to make smooth transitions as he fixates on objects at varying distances and in varying positions is checked. The child should be able to change his focus from object to object smoothly, without moving his head, and he should be able to maintain fixation without stress until the next object is presented.

The third area that is tested is stereopsis, the ability to see in the third dimension. For this evaluation a machine is needed. On some tests it is possible to get an actual percentage of stereoptic vision present, ranging from 0 to 100 per cent. By eight years of age it is expected that a youngster will have 100 per cent stereopsis.

The functions in the world that would be indicative of disorganization at this level overlap those of the bilateral stage to some degree. This is particularly true in the area of sports. If the child lacks stereopsis, he cannot judge where a ball is in space, and therefore, catching it or hitting it with a bat is difficult. If this child is motivated toward athletics, he will gravitate toward track, swimming, or wrestling, where he doesn't have to deal with an object in space.

In the classroom this child may have difficulty copying assignments from the blackboard in the appropriate length of time. He may omit part of what he is supposed to copy because he has trouble with accurate focusing as he moves from far-point to near-point distances. This child may also be using his finger to guide his eyes when he reads, although he is past the age where this is appropriate (eight years). The child with poor stereopsis is the one who can't walk by a table without knocking off anything that is hanging over the edge. He bumps into things because he really doesn't see where they are.

Interestingly enough this child may well be a runner; he is the one child who never walks from one place to another. It may be that his functional walk is poor but that when he runs, he goes into a good cross pattern, so that running is more efficient for him. He will, however, still bump into things.

As in the evaluation of other stages, it is necessary to look at the child's developmental history. Was he a late or an early walker? Did he walk on his tiptoes for an extended period of time? Did he bump into things a lot? We evaluate history, function in the world, and performance on the developmental tests appropriate for this stage.

The final stage of evaluation is to determine the degree to which the child has established laterality, or one-sidedness. Except for one test for the sighting eye (the eye that is preferred for a particular function), the evaluation is fairly simple. Which hand does the child use for skilled acts such as writing, cutting, tearing, throwing? Which foot does he use for kicking (punting), hopping? Which eye does he use for far-point tasks such as looking through a telescope or sighting with both eyes open? To test which is the sighting eye at near point (reading distance), the child, who is standing, is asked to look through a paper tube at an X marked on a paper that is on his desk. The child will naturally look with the sighting eye. The head posture when writing also gives information about which eye is the skilled eye.

One of the most important tests requires the use of a telebinocular. This test tells us which eye perceives better when both eyes are seeing. It is possible for a person who has 20/20 vision in each eye when they are measured separately to suppress an eye functionally to less than 20/20 vision when both eyes are seeing.

When all this information has been tabulated, the sensorimotor specialist has sufficient information about the degree to which the child has established laterality.

There are two different ways that a child will exhibit lack of organization at this level. Both are fairly common among the learning disabled population. One way is for the child to be mixed in handedness. The most flagrant example is the five-year-old who writes the first two letters of his name with one hand, then switches and writes the remaining letters with his other hand. More common, though, is the child who is mixed in skills; for example, he eats with one hand and writes with the other. The most frequent form of ambidexterity after eight years is performing small-muscle tasks, such as writing and eating, with one hand and large-muscle tasks, such as throwing, with the other hand.

Although there continues to be a lot of controversy over the implications of mixed dominance for learning disabilities, the fact remains that the problem exists within this population far too frequently for it to be ignored. It may be that one of the reasons why the mixed dominance characteristic (i.e., being right-eyed and left-handed or vice versa) fails to yield statistically significant results in research is that it is treated as an isolated factor rather than as part of a sequence of development. The child who exhibits developmental lags only in the area of laterality will perform better than the child who shows developmental lags in other areas as well. To combine children who have various problems including mixed dominance with those having only the problem of mixed dominance could statistically mask significant results.

There is no such thing as eye dominance. Nerve fibers from each eye go to both sides of the brain, so that one hemisphere cannot control one eye or receive all the impulses from it. We develop a preferred eye for different tasks. A right-handed individual will sight better with a rifle if he uses his right eye. But when the same person plays baseball or tennis, he must sometimes use his left eye to pick up the ball coming at him.

What the child needs to develop is strong binocularity and enough ease of *equal* use to choose whichever eye is appropriate for the task at hand. It has not been established that an individual prefers one eye for reading; the most efficient reader is the most *binocular*.

The child with laterality problems (right- or left-sidedness) is the child who never knows left from right. He is the child who forever has his shoes on the wrong feet. He also has trouble with reversals in reading. Sometimes even in speech, *b* and *d* are interchangeable, as are *was* and *saw*. The problem may be more subtle—for example, *left* may be seen as *felt*—but all this leads to much confusion in reading. This child may also have great difficulty developing a sight vocabulary (i.e., recognizing words on sight). Words he knew yesterday he can't recognize today.

In looking at the developmental history of this child in terms of handedness, the confusion may be obvious. Another factor that should be checked would be the parents' handedness. Is there left-handedness or ambidexterity in his family? This can give information that will prove helpful in the treatment.

Other tests that are not strictly developmental but that give added information in identifying inadequate or poor levels of function are:

Somersaults. Difficulty in doing these or falling over sideways would indicate balance problems and poor spatial orientation.

Kinesthetic integrity. The ability to move body parts on

touch indicates body awareness and sensorimotor integration.

Ability to balance on one foot and/or walk a balance beam. This test gives additional information on balance and spatial orientation. Balance problems often occur in tandem with auditory discrimination problems, speech articulation difficulties, and poor spelling and math.

Hopping on one foot. This tests development of this skill and gives indications of balance problems.

Skipping. The ability to skip shows skilled performance in cross-pattern movement and motor integration.

When the evaluator has checked all these developmental activities, functions, and skills, he or she should have enough information to put together an accurate picture of the child's difficulties and to locate them properly on his developmental profile. If, for instance, the evaluation reveals that reflexive and alternate one-sided functions are good and that the difficulties show up in the bilateral stage activities and relate to poor skills in binocularity and eye-hand coordination, then he or she will be able to pinpoint the developmental stage of the profile where the child is inadequately organized.

Once we have examined all the things that happen at various stages of development and the interactions of motor and sensory systems, we should then be able to make connections between, and inferences about, the lack of a skill at a higher level (e.g., reading and writing) and a difficulty with a developmental function at a lower level (e.g., creeping, tumbling, walking). These connections become the basis of further developmental evaluation and subsequent therapy.

THE TESTING PROCESS

We usually know which higher skills are lacking or poorly done. A child is brought to a developmental clinic because he can't read, write, or whatever, easily and well. What we need to know is *why* the child is having difficulty. A good kindergarten teacher can spot the children who are having problems and who will not make it in first grade, but that astute teacher will not know *why* this should be so. That is not within his or her province. Some special testing can be done in school, but much of it is not or cannot be done there. Thus, it may well require the experience of other disciplines to diagnose the child and to determine the *why*.

First we must be sure external stimuli are being received properly so that adequate processing can be performed. Therefore, the basic sensory functions of hearing, seeing, and tactility (touch) must be assessed. Evaluations must include observations of behavior in ordinary activity and surroundings as well as testing in isolated settings. And audiometer can be used to check the child's hearing to be sure it is within normal speech range. Next, a test of auditory discrimination should be done to ensure that he hears the difference in sounds. If *school, stool,* and *spool* all sound the same to him, it will certainly affect his auditory comprehension and spelling, and he may also be the kid who says, "I have to go to tool today." The child with an auditory problem may be hyperactive simply for that reason. If all the world of sounds comes in as a buzz, without differentiation, it creates confusion, and the usual defense is to make your own noise so that there is some contact with reality. A child with this problem usually goes around making noises, humming, screaming, "la la"ing, and generally driving those around him to distraction by constantly banging on things as he passes. He pounds on a wall, bangs on the desk, moves the chair, hits the table, reinforcing auditory inputs as if he is saying to himself, "I know where I am and that what's around me is real and is *there*."

The child who is oversensitive to sounds and hears everything simultaneously and at the same noise level may be driven to distraction by his auditory world. If he can't separate the hum of the fluorescent light, the cars going by outside, the noise from the playground, the plane flying overhead, two kids whispering in the back row, twenty pencils rustling on paper, and so on, how can he attend to what the teacher is saying? This is also the child who, if really interested in something such as watching a television show or model building, gets so engrossed in it that "the house could fall down around him, and he wouldn't know it." "I can call him twenty times, and he doesn't hear me. I have to go tap him on the shoulder to get his attention." In order to attend to what he wants to do, he *has* to shut out all that racket, and he learns to turn off his ears.

Vision must be evaluated for multiple functions. The child must have adequate visual acuity to see properly. He also must have smooth pursuits, (i.e., the ability of the eyes to track an object evenly, without jerkiness) in order to move easily across a line of print. And both eyes must be getting the same view at the same time and the same place. It must be noted that a child who has a visual problem usually doesn't know it. He's never known any other way of seeing things. If he has always had blurred vision or seen double, or if he has never had depth percep-

ocaatt

tion, he would not be aware that it's different from the way everyone else sees things.

SCREENING TESTS

When a child is not performing up to his or her potential, there are a variety of testing devices that are important in pinpointing the particular problem or problems. Following is a list of some devices.

Telebinocular

The telebinocular verifies functional evaluations and screens for organic visual problems. It tests gross binocularity, vertical and horizontal balance, and acuity. In addition, the telebinocular rules out suppression (i.e., the brain cutting off images from one eye to prevent double vision) and tests what one eye perceives when both eyes are seeing. It tests stereopsis as well as color blindness and figure-ground discrimination.

The telebinocular tests all these factors at both near point and far point and can be used to test fusion reserves and the ability to maintain binocularity for extended periods of time (e.g., reading time). The telebinocular evaluation is the basis for referral for a full visual work-up.

Audiometer

This tests for pure tone–hearing acuity and provides the basis for referral for a full hearing work-up by an audiologist.

Wepman Auditory Discrimination Test

This test evaluates the child's ability to hear the difference in sounds. If difficulties correlate with balance problems, the child may need a vestibular (balance mechanisms located in the middle ear) program. Difficulties detected through this test may also correlate with speech difficulties, and again a vestibular program (which strengthens and improves balance) is recommended (see Chapter 5).

If the results represent an erratic pattern of errors and do not correlate with other difficulties, this test may be the basis for a referral for impedence testing or for auditory perception testing. Impedence testing consists of checking blockage in the inner ear by measuring sound vibration in the eardrum. Auditory perception testing consists of testing the brain's interpretation of sounds.

Digit Span

The digit span test consists of asking a child to repeat orally a series of numbers or digits in sequence. The test builds from three digits to a maximum of nine. Then the child is tested for his ability to repeat them backward (i.e., in reverse order). This tests for attention and concentration.

Bender Gestalt Test and/or Beery Visual Motor Integration and/or Draw A Person

These are tests for figure copying and visual-motor integration. The Bender Gestalt Test consists of a series of cards, each of which contains geometric designs or figures that a child is asked to copy. The results of these tests may correlate with pursuits and convergence results on the bilateral level. They may correlate with the telebinocular findings and will probably be reflected in creeping.

The Interrelationship of Tests

Performance in the world is reflected in developmental testing, and each test correlates in some measure with other tests. For example, the child with a wide-based creep (i.e., hands and knees spread wide apart) will be underconvergent and will separate the figures on the

The manner in which the child is holding the paintbrush is an indication of fine motor difficulties, in this case inadequate finger dexterity. This could also relate to problems with buttoning, tying, handwriting, and other manipulative activities. (Photo: Ted Horowitz)

What does Johnnie *really* see? A child with visual problems may perceive the *b*'s in *bumble bee* as *d*'s, or he may perceive the words as grouped differently, for example, *si ton* for *sit on* or *abum bleb ee* for *bumble bee*. (Photo: Ted Horowitz)

The balance beam can be used in a number of ways for various types of problems. In this case pointing at one toe with the opposite finger while looking at both toe and finger as he walks improves this child's eye-hand coordination. This also improves finger-ground discrimination and depth perception because the child is putting his finger, the beam, and the floor into perspective. If the child is working only on balance problems, he should walk on the beam blindfolded and/or backward. (Photo: Ted Horowitz)

Darral Chapman and James Billy, sensorimotor therapists at the New York Institute for Child Development, swinging a child. This stimulates the child's balance mechanisms, which, in turn, improves his balance in normal activities such as walking, running, and riding a bicycle. And besides—it's fun! (Photo: Ted Horowitz)

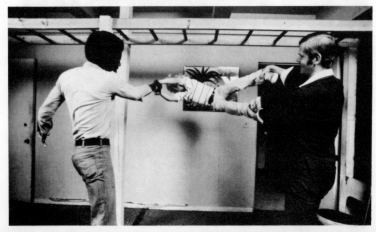

A child with poor control over eye movements uses the peg arc as a daily exercise. He moves the pegs, one by one, around the arc and down the middle to improve eye muscle control, convergence, and eye-hand coordination. This improved control will, in turn, improve accuracy of reading, will increase reading time, and will also help improve skills in ball sports. (Photo: Ted Horowitz)

A child with balance problems hangs upside down from the overhead ladder to stimulate his balance mechanisms. (Photo: Ted Horowitz)

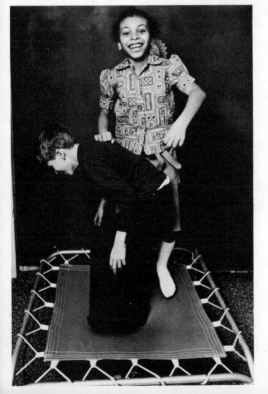

Jumping up and down on a trampoline improves balance and spatial orientation by increasing kinesthetic awareness. (Photo: Ted Horowitz)

Bender. Such a child probably walks with his head thrust forward in order to compensate for difficulties in focusing.

The child with a narrow-based creep (i.e., hands and knees close together) will often be overconvergent when tested for convergence with the telebinocular and will more than likely blend the geometric figures on the Bender. He will probably walk with his head thrust backward to compensate for focusing.

Difficulties on the Bender Gestalt Test, with eye-hand coordination, bilateral pursuits, convergence, and so on will be reflected in poor handwriting and general school performance.

CORRELATION WITH EDUCATIONAL TESTS

The child who starts out reading well on the Gray Oral Reading Tests or on a reading comprehension test and who falls apart after the second or third paragraph probably has poor fusion reserves and is losing binocularity. That means that the brain is not easily able to hold the single image it puts together from the impulses from the right and left eyes.

The child who has high word recognition, high to average word meaning, either high or low comprehension, and low speed and accuracy has binocularity and tracking problems. If this child follows the written word with his finger or pencil, he is telling you he needs a bilateral visual program because he is performing a bilateral function: tracking with the aid of his finger. Such a program develops the ability of the two eyes to work together without the aid of finger or pencil.

If a child has high word recognition, high to average speed and accuracy, and high to average word meaning but low comprehension, he may have binocularity and convergence problems and should be on a bilateral program. His comprehension is low because all his energies are going into keeping his eyes focused and he can't pay attention to what he is reading.

Math and spelling difficulties are basically reflections of poor stereopsis. This results in poor ability to see depth and also to know where one is in space. Poor stereopsis may also cause balance problems. Therefore, the child needs a combination vestibular (balance) and bilateral program.

In all these reading problems, the child is functioning under great visual stress, which is transformed to physical stress. This stimulates a biochemical stress reaction, which effectively lowers the blood sugar level. (Therefore, in addition to any sensorimotor program these children should also have a nutritional-dietary program, which will be discussed in Chapter 6.) In fact, low blood sugar can be diagnosed through a visual work-up, and it is a fact that with low blood sugar, accommodation of the lens in the eye may become three times slower than normal.

The next step after evaluation of the child's sensorimotor difficulties is a prescription for therapy or a program of treatment to restore the child to full functioning. However, before we proceed to a discussion of the modes of treatment that follow proper diagnosis (see Chapters 5 and 6), it may be helpful to review the relationship between functioning in the world (i.e., school) and the developmental stages described in this chapter.

NORMAL DEVELOPMENT AND EXPECTED PERFORMANCE

Although we have previously listed functional and educational warning signals, there are normal developmental signposts that can be considered normal or expected at various ages. The following is a breakdown of expected performance according to age and grade:

AGE	GRADE	EXPECTED PERFORMANCE
5	K	Dominance not established; stuttering; reversals; mirror writing (i.e., writing backwards); no skipping for boys, some for girls; no shoe tying, especially with boys; abnormal pencil grasp; hopping only on one foot; in visual evaluation, when following a circle, the child's eyes move in a square; convergence lost at two to three inches from the eye; telebinocular is invalid at this age for all visual testing except that of two-eyed vision; body awareness; good creeping.
6	1st	Good creeping; skipping for girls, not yet for boys; diminished or stopped reversals or mirror writing; shoe tying; pencil grasp closer to normal; in visual evaluation, when following a circle, the child's eyes move in a square on only one side; convergence to within two inches of the eye; body awareness (unilateral kinesthetic integrity); beginning of directionality; telebinocular valid for all visual testing except seeing in the third dimension; acuity depends on directionality; auditory discrimination becomes more refined; knows alphabet and does some reading; coloring within lines with consistent stroke direction; can follow rules for games.
7	2nd	Dominance established; no stuttering but some hesitation; skipping; no reversals or

AGE   GRADE   EXPECTED PERFORMANCE

inversions; all visual tests valid on tele-binocular; directionality and space concepts are established; able to organize materials (e.g., work on paper); time, number, size concepts established; in visual evaluation, the child's eyes should follow the circle perfectly on pursuits; convergence to within one inch of the eyes; depth perception established; no gross awkwardness; cross-pattern walking and good creeping.

7½   Body awareness with cross-lateral movements (i.e., right leg and left arm move at same time, and vice versa.)

7½–8   Hopping, skipping, jumping, and cortical opposition should be established.

8   3rd   All systems should be intact; able to travel independently around school and assume responsibility; telling of time and days and months; in visual evaluation, the child's eyes should follow the circle perfectly on pursuits; convergence to within one inch of the eyes; good reading; should receive and understand directions; should repeat 80 per cent of a second grade story in sequence; able to speak in ten- to twelve-word sentences with good structure.

One factor that should be mentioned in the context of this discussion of diagnosis is that hyperactivity and learning disabilities affect boys in a much higher ratio than girls. Eight out of every ten children seen at the

New York Institute for Child Development are boys. This higher male proportion is reported in other clinics and in research. The best explanation is that males are an endangered species at birth compared with females. There are twenty diseases that males up to age eight are subject to that females are not. Perhaps more important, in the male the language side of the brain (left hemisphere) is inferior to the nonlanguage side of the brain (right hemisphere). This difference is constant, regardless of age.

The female brain has superior language capabilities, and females have more neuroanatomical (relating to the anatomy of the central nervous system) support on the left side of the brain. Females develop at a more rapid growth rate than males and are not subject to the same risks as males. Consequently, in the male the ability to understand language, to read, and to write is more subject to difficulty.

V

Treatment: Sensorimotor Therapy

This chapter is concerned with one aspect of the learning disabled child's problems: sensorimotor development. Having a thorough diagnostic work-up on a child is only the first step. The parent then needs to find the appropriate treatment. This treatment should logically follow from the information obtained in the diagnostic procedure. Far too often, it seems, even after a good evaluation of a child's problem, many of the signposts of causal factors such as perceptual problems, eye-hand coordination problems, and balance problems, are ignored. Treatment becomes merely more concentrated training of the skills that initially were identified as inadequate instead of a strengthening of basic developmental level skills that are weak or nonexistent.

The obvious objective of any treatment is to improve the child's functioning in the world (reading, writing, and so on). Like evaluation, treatment can be aimed either at correcting the *skills* or at correcting the *cause*. If the evaluation basically defined the behaviors or skills that were inadequate in the child's performance, then the treatment would logically be defined in terms of these behaviors. This leads directly to such treatments as drugs for hyperactivity or tutoring for poor reading skills. However, these modalities of treatment do not address the basic condition or cause, and therefore they are not effective.

Take, for example, a child who is having difficulty reading. The diagnosis reveals that he has poor phonic skills and an inadequate sight vocabulary along with poor auditory and visual perception skills. At this point it would make sense that the poor auditory and visual perception might well be contributing factors in the child's inability to learn to read. A recommendation of tutoring, with the objective being to teach the child the skills he hasn't learned, would be inappropriate. Assuming he has had the same educational exposure as the other children in his class, there must be something that is interfering with his ability to learn. It would make more sense to pursue the area of auditory and visual perception skills. Distorted or inadequate perception could certainly make the sophisticated task of reading difficult. If these perceptual skills are improved, teaching of the reading skills would be more effective.

If the area of perceptual skills is examined, which is a step in the right direction, it may be determined that the child has poor binocularity (i.e., he cannot focus both eyes properly). This could create problems in reading; the child may see double or fuzzy images, making what he perceives difficult for him to interpret. Such an experience would be particularly true if his binocularity breaks down as he tires. Quite often a child may perform well one day and perform the next day as if he had never learned the skills. This behavior is confusing to parents and teacher alike. It is also frustrating to the child, a fact that is often overlooked.

What is to be done about the child's poor binocularity? Once again there are choices to be made. It is possible that the child can do eye exercises that may improve his binocularity. However, just as parents should be interested in why the child can't read, not just in the fact that he can't read, they should be interested in why the child doesn't have good binocularity. If this is determined in the diagnosis, then treatment should begin with the cause.

As you recall, in Chapter 3 we outlined the developmental sequence and discussed the relationship between the stages of mobility and visual skills. If the cause of the child's poor binocularity can be related to overall poor bilateral skills, then it may be possible to identify the reason for the lack of development of binocularity as insufficient opportunity to creep during development. For this child the initial treatment for his reading difficulty would be developmental exercises at the creeping level.

It is rare that a child has a single problem with a single cause. More often there are clusters of inappropriate behaviors. For example, the child mentioned with poor binocularity probably had more difficulties than a simple inability to learn to read. The child with poor binocularity often has a short attention span. This may be the result of the difficulty he has focusing both eyes on the printed page. Frequently he stares out the window to ease the stress. This child will often have poor handwriting, and he may be poor at ball sports, both of which require good eye-hand skills. A child's total functioning must be assessed in this way. Treatment should be developmentally based. Thus, when a child is inadequate in a cluster of skills, it is necessary to reinforce the developmental stage at which those skills developed.

In the long run this is more efficient than trying to teach the skills separately. Thus, the treatment prescribed should work up through developmental stages, with exercises plugged in where appropriate (i.e., where the developmental evaluation indicates a need for reinforcement), so that the child can perform higher skills such as reading and writing.

There are many exercises, games, and techniques for developmental reinforcement, and many of them are being used by various professionals and facilities around the country. Two important questions must be asked about these activities: Where do they fit into the developmental schema? What function will they reinforce? To give a child an exercise to do that is on too high a level (or too low a level) is a disservice. To "teach" splinter skills is to ignore the problem. To work on pencil-paper tasks when the problem is binocularity is piling more frustration on the child and more stress on his visual system. An exercise program must be geared to fit the needs of the child where his dysfunction begins.

All movement is dependent on balance mechanisms, vision, and proprioception. The latter, often referred to as the *sixth sense*, is the feeling of position and movement that makes possible both the assuming and maintenance of a position and the repetition of that movement or position. All three receive stimuli that the brain interprets and translates into motion and its control. The accuracy of all movements depends on the sorting of these stimuli and the adjustments made to them. For example, the ability to write involves a number of different functions. It involves the proper positioning of the hand and the movement of the hand. It involves the eyes, and it involves communication from the brain to the hand to form letters and words in a prescribed manner. We must examine an activity to determine what systems it may be affecting and how and then place it in the developmental schema. Every activity should have more than one component. A motor exercise should have a visual aspect or an auditory-balance factor and/or a balance experience or a combination of all three. Every activity necessarily has a tactile input in that the brain is being made aware of what the body is doing through proprioception.

Certainly people can cope without all of these, as a blind person does, but substitute information must be depended on, and accuracy of movement is definitely affected until a great deal of repetition and learning have taken place. More problems arise when all systems are operating but one or more is working poorly and therefore supplying inaccurate information. What we must do is work with those systems to improve the quality of sensory information and therefore to improve the accuracy of motor control.

If a child demonstrates any difficulties with balance or related functions, then a program of exercises to stimulate and improve balance is appropriate. This stimulation can be very simple and can be fun for the child. It could include rolling from side to side, somersaults, hanging upside down from a bar or jungle gym, or simply turning the head from side to side while lying on the stomach. Such exercises stimulate the balance mechanism, which is located in the inner ear. When this is accomplished, various activities can be used to refine balance and balance retrieval (the ability to regain balanced position): walking on a narrow beam, balancing on a round-bottomed disk, maintaining balance on a large uneven surface on all fours. Many, many games can be devised for this type of stimulation and training if we keep in mind what it is we are trying to accomplish.

If problems are identified as significant in the unilateral stage (i.e., the use of right hand and right eye), it is appropriate to give an exercise appropriate to that stage, such as crawling, if the child can do it. If he cannot, he may have to begin with flip-flops (for complete instructions, see "Flip-flops" at the end of this chapter) and then progress to crawling itself. He may have an eye exercise at this level that would be similar to the test: following an object with the eye and hand on only one side of his body at a time.

If difficulties are identified at the bilateral stage (e.g., poor binocularity, poor eye-hand function, poor handwriting), reinforcement should be programmed at that level. An example would be creeping, which is specifically designed to improve finger dexterity and smooth body movement, as well as binocularity and therefore depth perception. Other bilateral activities, such as tracking a moving object with both eye and hand, may be given, depending on what specifically needs reinforcement.

For example, for higher-level reinforcement for the clumsy runner with poor stereopsis, we may again use a balance beam and a structured cross-pattern movement (for complete instructions, see "Cross-pattern Walking" at the end of this chapter). An overhead ladder can be very useful; the child swings from rung to rung, hand over hand, looking at each rung and placing his hand on it. This can improve eye-hand coordination and stereopsis and is an excellent fitness exercise as well.

We may reinforce hopping and skipping skills where necessary. The most important considerations in selecting exercise activities are: what functions need to be corrected or improved, at what neurological level or stage the dysfunctions occur, and which technique is best to change a function in the shortest length of time.

It is also important to be aware that developmental reinforcements can be telescoped. Not all functions at one level need to be perfected before the next level can be incorporated. A child may be on a principally bilateral program with one unilateral reinforcement exercise. For example, he may be doing creeping, peg arc, jumping jacks, cross-pattern walking, and both unilateral and bilateral tracking exercises (for complete instructions, see the exercise sections at the end of this chapter).

The child with sensorimotor deficiencies will profit very little from traditional treatments such as tutoring, counseling, and drugs. All these at best will establish a mere level of survival. We have to consider seriously whether this can be justified if we are dealing with a child whose potential to contribute to society is much greater than merely surviving. The child who has been identified as bright enough to cope with the regular school system and has had the same opportunity as his successful peers to learn the fundamentals but hasn't grasped the material is saying, "There is something wrong with me, something wrong with the way I perceive the world. It doesn't make the same kind of sense to me that it does to everyone else."

This child often exhibits developmental deficits that an evaluation and treatment program (as identified in this chapter and in Chapters 3 and 4) can remove, thereby enhancing his learning process. As the level of developmental functioning improves, the related functioning in the world improves. This does not preclude the possibility of tutoring or some other supportive treatment at some time. However, it is a much more profitable and rewarding process to tutor a child in reading whose visual perceptual skills are at least equivalent to those of a six-year-old than to try to teach these sophisticated skills to a child who is visually functioning at a three-year level. Again, and uppermost, what needs to be done and how it can be done most effectively and efficiently are important.

Following are three case studies that illustrate the types of programs that apply to specific problems, why any particular exercise is used, and how developmental stages apply to functional difficulties in daily activities.

Tom, who is seven years old, was brought to the New York Institute because of his parents' concern with his coordination and learning difficulties.

His evaluation revealed that because of balance problems, perhaps resulting from immobility while wearing a body brace as an infant, he could neither hop nor skip, his movements were poorly controlled, and he was a toe walker. Fine motor skills were poor, and he held a pencil in a fisted grasp. He had very immature oculomotor skills and was underconvergent, which means his two eyes were not able to focus properly. In brief, this means that although he had 20/20 vision, his eyes were not working together properly and he could not focus them effectively for near-point work such as reading.

When we designed his program, we kept in mind the fact that function determines structure. He had tight heel cords that were the *result*, not the cause, of the way he was walking. Every step was, in essence, a resistance exercise to the calf muscle, resulting in increased strength and tightening. To lengthen heel cords surgically in an instance such as this is self-defeating; six months later he would be right back where he started. However, by having Tom crawl (swimming style), every time he bends his knee and hip, he reflexly pulls his foot up; this stretches the calf muscle and over a period of time lengthens it and strengthens the muscle that raises the front of his foot and toes. At first Tom only pulled with his hands, so we had him put his hands behind his back and use only his legs and feet.

Tom was also given two-eyed pursuits to smooth his uncoordinated eye movements and somersaults, rolling, and hanging upside down by his knees for balance. Four months later he was walking heel and toe consistently and was falling much less. Everyone, including his teachers, saw a big improvement in his coordination. At that point we cut crawling time in half and added creeping for binocularity and cortical opposition, the balance beam for refinement of balance stimulation, and the peg arc for convergence and eye-hand coordination.

Tom is currently on that regimen and is improving continually.

Mike, age seven, came to us with difficulties similar to Tom's except that he was overconvergent at far point; that is, his eyes were unable to focus on objects at twenty feet distant. He had an oculomotor age equivalent of a two-and-a-half-year-old but was not a toe walker. For his visual problem we gave him flip-flops as one of his exercises. Each time he turns his head, he reads a word card someone is holding for him. This stimulates use of alternate sides of the body and by having the eyes move from one side to another should help pull the eyes out of overconvergence. Mike also does pursuits with one eye at a time. We're beginning to notice changes. As soon as both eyes start working together, we'll change him to a bilateral program to reinforce the use of the two eyes and therefore stereopsis.

Dan, a thirteen-year-old, is representative of a large percentage of the children we see. The use of large-muscle groups, such as those in the arms and legs, are fine, as are small-muscle groups, such as fingers and eyes. He appears to have all the skills necessary for reading and schoolwork. He is not a behavior problem, but he was failing in school with an IQ of over 130! In oculomotor testing his pursuits were very jerky, causing him to skip words and lines, lose his place often, reread the same line, and so on. Also, on visual testing he was underconvergent at near point, and he had to put greater effort into focusing his eyes on the page. This extra effort wasted energy that would have enabled him to read efficiently. Like many of these children, Dan begins losing comprehension as soon as the stress point is reached. This combination of problems is borne out by reading scores. Dan had a four-year spread between word recognition (tenth grade level) and speed and accuracy (sixth grade level).

Dan's exercises are geared specifically for binocularity and smooth oculomotor control. He began with creeping, pursuits, binocular cross-pattern walking on a balance beam, and figure-ground discrimination. After two weeks Dan's pursuits were smoother, so we added a peg arc exercise. This makes the eyes work in a very orderly and structured pattern, smoothing out the movements, as well as improving convergence. After one month there were improvements in visual testing, so we cut Dan's creeping time in half and added accommodation exercises with pegs for further oculomotor control.

Dan is seeing improvement in schoolwork and is making fewer mistakes when reading music. At the end of only two months Dan's reading is faster and better, and his grades have improved.

DIRECTIONS FOR SPECIFIC
DEVELOPMENTAL SENSORIMOTOR ACTIVITIES

The following pages present directions for teaching specific sensorimotor activities that have been previously discussed and drawings that demonstrate how they should be done. This outline has been prepared by the New York Institute for Child Development in order to systematize its diagnostic and treatment modalities.

STRUCTURED CRAWLING

Crawling is a motor activity that involves moving

across the floor on the stomach, using both the arms and the legs in a cross pattern. To do structured crawling:

1. The child lies on the floor on his stomach. He should wear as few clothes as possible and no shoes.

2. The opposite arm and leg are bent upward; the head is turned toward the extended arm, the eyes looking at the hand.

3. The child propels himself forward by pushing with the foot and pulling with the extended hand.

4. As the child moves forward, he turns his head to the opposite side and brings up the other arm. The descending hand sweeps from palm down to palm up, coming down just under his chest.

5. As the leg that is pushing straightens, the opposite leg bends up, ready to push.

EXAMPLE: The child's head is turned to the right; the right arm is bent and extended comfortably forward; the

CRAWLING

right leg is straight; the left leg is bent; the left arm is straight down at the side, with the palm of the hand up. As the left foot pushes and the right hand pulls, the head begins to turn, and the pattern is shifted. However, each hand in turn now moves under the body as the child moves. The child looks at the extended hand.

STRUCTURED CREEPING

Creeping is an important step in motor development. It develops good bilateral functioning. The following are the specific elements your child should include in structured creeping:

1. The opposite hand and knee move at the same time:
   a. right hand with left knee
   b. left hand with right knee
2. The moving hand and knee should touch the floor at the same time.
3. The knee should come up to gently meet the back of the wrist of the stationary hand. For example, when the left hand moves forward with the right knee, the right knee touches the floor *and* the back of the right wrist.
4. The hands should rest flat on the floor about shoulder width apart, fingers loosely together and pointed forward.
5. The child should lift the knees and drag the toes.
6. The child should always look at the hand that is in front. The head should tilt slightly toward that hand.

CREEPING

FLIP-FLOPS

Flip-flops are a primary motor activity observed in infants. They stimulate the alternate use of body sides and are essential for later bilateral skills.

To do flip-flops correctly:

1. The child lies comfortably on the floor on his stomach. He should wear a minimum amount of clothing and no shoes.

2. The head is turned to one side.

3. The arm and leg on the same side to which the head is turned are bent upward. The palm of the hand is down flat on the floor.

4. The child looks at the hand on that side.

5. The child then turns his head to the opposite side, shifting (reversing) the body position.

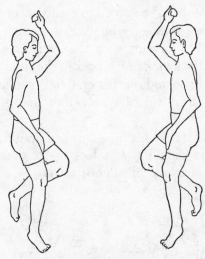

FLIP-FLOPS
(child lying on stomach)

6. All the body parts should move at the same time; forehead, toes, and hands should lightly touch the surface of the floor as the movement occurs.

7. The hand sweeps down from the palm down to palm up.

Flip-flops may also be done in cross pattern. To do so, the child should follow the instructions for crawling, but without propelling his body forward. That is, the child should remain in one place while doing cross-pattern flip-flops.

Cross-Pattern Walking

Structured walking is an exercise that facilitates the easy gait of natural cross-pattern walking. To do cross-pattern walking properly:

1. The child stands with feet comfortably apart (approximately six inches), with hands relaxed at the sides of the body.

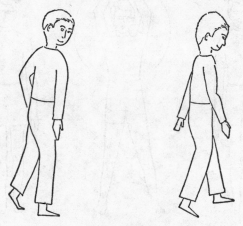

CROSS-PATTERN WALKING

2. To begin, the child takes one step forward. At the same time as he steps, he points the index finger of the opposite hand to that foot. The child looks down and sees both his finger and his toe. The hand that is not pointing moves behind the body.

3. On the next step, the movement is reversed.

4. Walking should be done at an even pace.

JUMPING JACKS

Jumping jacks is a motor activity designed to increase body awareness and spatial orientation. To do jumping jacks correctly:

1. The child stands with his feet together and his arms at his sides.

2. To begin, the child jumps so that his feet are parallel and spread two feet apart and his arms are extended

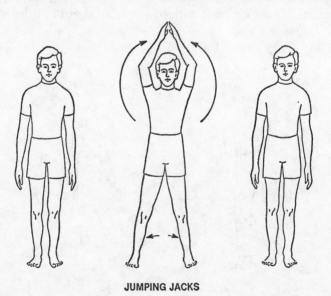

JUMPING JACKS

overhead; his hands should meet in clapping position. These movements should be simultaneous.

3. The child then returns his arms and legs to the position in step 1.

4. The child should repeat this sequence 20 times.

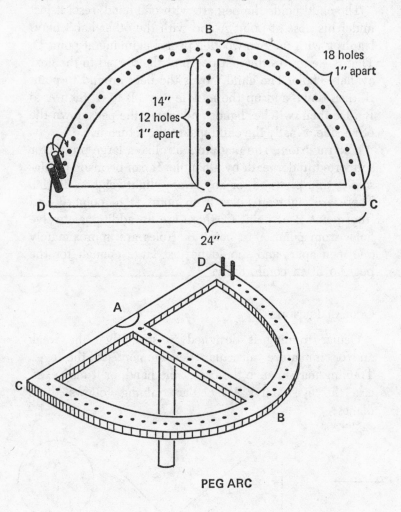

PEG ARC

Peg Arc

The peg arc is a simple apparatus designed to help the two eyes to work together.

The child holds the peg arc with one hand, rests it just under his nose at point A and with the other hand plays leapfrog with the two wooden pegs, beginning at point D. That is, he moves the first peg past the second to the next available hole. The child moves the pegs around to point B, then down and up the middle row (B to A, then A to B). He then switches hands and moves the pegs down the other side. Finally the child makes the return trip.

CONSTRUCTION: The peg arc looks like a large protractor supported underneath by a handle. It can be made of Masonite, thin plywood, or any strong, lightweight material. There are eighteen holes from point D to point B and from point B to point C; there are an additional twelve holes from point A to point B. Holes are approximately one inch apart and should be just large enough for the pegs to fit in comfortably.

Ocular Pursuits

Ocular training is designed to strengthen the weak and/or immature muscular development of the eyes. Training may involve the use of the hand, or it may exercise the eyes only. All ocular training follows these planes:

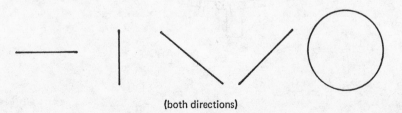

(both directions)

1. *To Do Monocular (One-eyed) Pursuits:*

a. Child covers left eye with left hand, follows pencil (penlight, ball) that the therapist is moving on all planes for the prescribed amount of time, which varies depending on the child's needs. Do the same with the other eye.

b. Repeat (a), but child follows the pencil (penlight, ball) with the index finger (arm extended), as well as with the eye, for the prescribed amount of time.

EXAMPLE: Left eye is covered. Right arm is extended, finger pointed at the pencil. The child then looks down his arm, over his finger, and to the pencil. The child follows the pencil as it moves with both his eye and his finger. (*Note:* If his arm becomes fatigued, the child may do one plane with one eye and hand and then switch to the other eye and hand on the same plane until all planes are done.)

2. *To Do Binocular (Two-eyed) Pursuits:*

a. Have both eyes follow the finger and the pencil; use the dominant hand to follow all planes.

b. Have both eyes follow the object without the use of hands on all planes.

3. *Convergence.* Bring the pencil (penlight) slowly in to tip of the nose. Hold it there for as long as possible, building up to twenty seconds. Bring the pencil out again. The child should keep his eyes on the pencil at *all* times.

4. *Marsden Ball:*

a. A ball about the size of a tennis ball is suspended from the ceiling to arm's length above the floor. The child lies on his back, with his head directly under the ball. The therapist moves the ball in the directions for monocular or binocular pursuits. The child's head should remain fixed at all times.

b. Tapping the ball. The child either sits or stands, and the ball is at the child's eye level. It is rotated gently and is tapped by the child with each hand alternately.

LENGTH OF SENSORIMOTOR PROGRAMS

When a child masters the activity he is working on and it carries over to the expected function in the world, he can then move to the next level of activity. It is not uncommon (as stated) to have a child on several levels of activities at one time. Developmental stages overlap, and all the areas do not finish at the same time. So you might be reinforcing an activity at one level while starting another activity at a different level. For example, you might be reinforcing monocular pursuits while beginning a bilateral program with creeping and the peg arc.

When the child performs all cortical activities well and they carry over to their expected functions in the world, the child has completed his sensorimotor program.

NOTE WELL: If a child performs an activity, such as creeping well, but he can't maintain convergence or cortical opposition (which is what creeping is for), he still needs a creeping program to achieve binocularity.

SAMPLE SCHOOL MODULE

Although each child should be treated as an individual, entire classes can be put on a sensorimotor program. Here is a sample school module that a teacher can use or adapt to fit his or her needs:

Have the children walk around the top of the sandbox or any other piece of balance equipment; then have them creep ten to twelve feet to an obstacle course. The obstacle course could be a series of one-foot blocks spaced one foot apart. Have the children go up and over the blocks and then roll or somersault five to six feet to the Lite-Brite, a commercial game (manufactured by Hasbro) in which pegs are inserted into a board and a picture is illuminated when enough pegs are inserted). Each child should insert two to three pegs.

Play a game of Simon says. If possible, have the children go to the jungle gym and do hand-over-hand activities. Play a game of accommodation rocks (the teacher says, "I see something red," and the child must identify it without moving his head), or team up the children to do visual tracking with mirrors.

Play a game of body alphabet, in which the child forms letters by moving his or her arms and legs. If activities are in the classroom or are modified to be done in the classroom, blackboard or pencil-paper activities can be incorporated.

Peg arc activities should be done just before the break.

Teach each exercise (creeping, visual tracking, hand-over-hand activities) before having the children attempt them. Make sure the exercises are done properly. The more frequently they are performed, the more facile the children will become at performing them.

VI

Nutrition, Behavior, Learning

There is increasing recognition among physicians, nutritionists, and parents who are trying to cope with hyperactive and learning disabled children that nutritional status plays an important role. Many of the problems that these children (and their families) suffer from may well be related to the food they do or do not eat.

Chapters 3, 4, and 5 were primarily concerned with the diagnosis and treatment of sensorimotor developmental problems of hyperactive and learning disabled children. This chapter is devoted to the evaluation and treatment of biochemical, nutritional, and dietary problems of that same population. The relationship between the child's biochemical life and his functional performance is very important. Blood tests reveal that 75 per cent of hyperactive–learning disabled children have low blood sugar and/or allergies.[1] These disorders indicate stress in the body and affect the visual functioning of a child.

Chronically undernourished animals and humans have shown evidence of physiological and biochemical changes in the central nervous system and brain. Inadequate nutrient intake affects the development of the brain most crucially during the period of rapid growth. In humans this critical period occurs during the last three months of pregnancy and the first six months of infancy. Furthermore, 90 per cent of the total growth of the brain takes place during the first three years of life! Evidence is accumulating detailing the influence of nutritional status on neuromuscular functions, behavior, and intelligence. Dr. Myron Winick and Dr. A. Noble have demonstrated that undernutrition during these critical periods of brain cell growth produces a reduced number of brain cells and a smaller brain size. At this time the myelin sheath that protects the nerve fibers is also being formed. Thus, you are what you eat and what your mother ate and even what your grandmother and great-grandmother ate because the genes that carry the pattern for development may pass on the effects of poor eating habits.

But what happens at birth? After the structure of the nervous system has been laid down, the ability to develop and respond to neuromuscular and environmental stimuli will still be affected by foods eaten. The extent of any developmental disorders depends on the stage of development in which the undernutrition occurs and on the severity and the duration of the deprivation. F. Monkeberg noted a lack of motor development (psychomotor retardation) in 220 preschool children who were not receiving optimal amounts of essential nutrients.[2] Reduced attention span and intellectual ability, lack of emotional stability, and decreased accuracy in performance involving neuromuscular coordination have also been observed. A study conducted on students at the University of Minnesota in 1960 showed that their ability to think was reduced when they were kept on a nutritionally poor diet, that is, a diet characterized by a lack or imbalance of proteins, fats, carbohydrates, and vitamins.[3]

Specific nutrient deficiencies will produce specific deficiency symptoms, some of which are familiar as symptoms of hyperactivity and learning disorders. A deficiency of thiamine (vitamin B_1) may produce irritability, nervousness, and even increased sensitivity to noise. If niacin is inadequate in the diet, lethargy and anxiety—and in severe cases, confusion—may result. Iron deficiency, unfortunately prevalent in the United States, as shown by the U. S. Public Health Service *Ten-State Nutrition Survey, 1968–1970,*[4] is associated with decreased ability to concentrate, decreased persistence and a reduction in activity along with an increase in irritability. A teacher's observation that a child is "not meeting his potential, not motivated" is often a clue to the presence of iron deficiency.

Clearly, undernutrition adversely affects performance. Measurement of these effects is not simple, but lack of energy and difficulty in concentration may easily create long-term problems. Poor nutrition not only may damage the central nervous system physiologically and biochemically but also may result in severe learning disabilities that lead to poor interactions with other people and the environment. A vicious cycle then presents itself: A child who tires easily, is irritable, and cannot and does not attract normal interrelationships becomes a more isolated, a more irritable, a more frustrated, and a more difficult child with less and less motivation.

The parents' old refrain of "eat, eat" holds true but with a few caveats. The kinds of food and the amounts of food matter! Less well documented but increasingly evident is the result of overnutrition (excess or imbalance of one or more nutrients). This would include excess intake of proteins, fats, carbohydrates, vitamins, and minerals. (See end of chapter for chart indicating normal nutritional needs.)

The large intake of sugar in the United States is a hazard against which many nutritionists have long been preaching. Too often a diet high in concentrated sweets (refined sugar)—sodas, jellies, fruit punches, flavored gelatin, cupcakes, cookies, ad nauseam—is low in foods with the essential nutrients. Such a diet takes the child back to square one: chronic undernutrition. Parents, doctors, and dentists admonish, "No sweets, they're not good for you." Yet mothers, fathers, and grandparents all continue to serve candy, soda, and cakes at home, and doctors and even dentists continue to offer lollipops to "good little girls and boys." Teachers tear their hair—these children are impossible to teach!—yet they continue to bring in such "treats" as jelly beans, gumdrops, and candy canes.

Our observations at the New York Institute for Child Development indict sugar as a critical culprit in producing symptoms of hyperactivity and learning disorders. A survey of the diet analyses of hundreds of these children indicates that the majority eat a high percentage of concentrated sweets. Most have difficulty metabolizing carbohydrates. The basic causes of their behavioral problems (irritability, inability to sit still, short attention span, temper tantrums) are not definitively known, but, again, their high intake of sugar is certainly another clue that points to nutrition counseling for hyperactive children.

Another area of nutrition to be considered is the intake of artificial colors and flavors and the preservatives of BHT and BHA. Dr. Ben Feingold has commented extensively on his observations of hyperactive children when these additives are eliminated from the diet. It may well be that some children are sensitive to these particular additives. Certainly, as more research is conducted on them, the concern over their adverse effects on everyone escalates. It is no doubt advisable to eliminate these from foods as much as possible. Dr. Feingold has also reported on salicylates (found in particular fruits and vegetables and in aspirin) as being a cause of hyperactivity. This appears to be an individual sensitivity that needs to be determined along with food allergies. Unfortunately, Dr. Feingold has not given weight to what seems to be the most harmful element for many hyperactive children: sugar.

Until recent years nutrient intake studies were the prime concern in evaluating dietary habits. But it has become evident that more complex factors are involved. For example, different kinds of carbohydrates react differently in the body. Refined sugar is rapidly absorbed into the bloodstream and can trigger a hyperactive syndrome. In contrast, more complex carbohydrates (such as starches) are better metabolized because they feed into the bloodstream at a slower rate and take longer to be digested.

The utilization of carbohydrates by the body is another example of the complexity of nutritional needs. The B vitamins are essential for energy to be produced in that process. At the same time no amount of B vitamins can produce energy without carbohydrates. The proper amounts and proper proportions of nutrients are essential for such body functions to take place.

All these areas need to be explored in depth in order to properly assess a child's nutritional needs.

The nutrition program at the New York Institute for Child Development is geared to each child's specific biochemical problems. Working within the framework of the child's biochemical disorders, we prescribe a diet that aims to alleviate these disorders while ensuring that the child has a diet that includes all the essential nutrients.

NUTRITIONAL ASSESSMENT

How are a child's nutritional status and problems determined?

First, a *medical history* of the child is necessary. This includes height-weight records, illnesses, sleep habits, medications, allergies, and prenatal history.

Height-weight records. Facts of interest include birth weight and specific problems at delivery, including toxemias, jaundice, and/or anemia.

Maternal weight gain. It is important to gain some knowledge of maternal eating patterns during pregnancy. A high weight gain is often invalid, however, because it may not necessarily indicate that a pregnant woman was getting all essential nutrients.

Infant feeding patterns. Was the infant breast-fed, or were different formulas, which may often cause allergies, used? Special considerations are made if the baby was breast-fed. Occasionally, when a mother eats an excess of one food, such as nuts or bananas, during pregnancy, the possibility exists that by some unexplained mechanism the foods can pass through the placenta to the fetus and cause allergy development when this food is introduced into the child's diet.

Sometimes a pediatrician will switch an infant's formula from cow's milk to another kind of milk or delete one ingredient without the infant's mother understanding what is being done and why. All milk (i.e., soybean milk, goat's milk, or cow's milk) can cause allergies. Whether it does or not depends on which kind of milk is affecting the child adversely. It is possible to be allergic to cow's milk or soybean milk but not allergic to goat's milk.

If one food in the infant's diet is suspected, allergy can be verified by simply omitting the food in *all* forms for at least fourteen days. If, after two weeks, the child seems much better, the food is added to the diet again to see if the symptoms recur.

Infants' problems. Colic, diarrhea, poor sleeping habits,

constant crying seizures, and other problems that infants
face can be important indicators of discomfort. These
symptoms often result from allergies to milk or ingredients in infants' foods. Doctors may be limited in knowledge regarding nutrition, may be unfamiliar with these
nutritional problems, and are often unequipped to handle
them properly. Doctors may assure mothers that foods
may be added even if allergic responses were experienced
the first time. "They will outgrow it" is a typical diagnosis
and one of which mothers should be aware.

Late bed-wetting, up to eighteen years of age for example, is a symptom we see in 20 per cent of our children.
Dr. William Crook,[5] a pediatric allergist, explains that
this symptom is a result of allergies. According to Dr.
Crook, eating foods that one is allergic to causes spasms.
In the head, fluid will leak out, and the brain may swell,
resulting in a throbbing headache. The same spasms in
the bladder muscle prevent the bladder from holding the
normal quantity of urine. This may mean more frequent
urinating during the day or wetting the bed at night.
Where this has been the case, a diet with more regular
feeding patterns, higher amounts of protein, lower
amounts of carbohydrates, and in some cases, more specific dietary eliminations has helped 85 per cent of these
children to control the problem.

Allergies do not always manifest themselves in eczema,
wheezing, or bellyaches. Perhaps the behavioral problems
we see are also a manifestation of allergies caused by
foods that for some reason are not handled successfully
by the body. Elimination diets prove successful within as
short a time period as two weeks when the proper food or
substance is eliminated. If it works and behavior and
physical complaints are relieved, it's worth a try. But
skilled analysis is required to eliminate the culprit, and
this can be difficult.

If an infant was sensitive to corn, this means that corn and corn products (i.e., cornmeal, corn oil, corn syrup, and cornstarch) must be eliminated. If it was milk, then milk, butter, cheese, cream, yogurt, nonfat dairy solids, whey, and so on must be eliminated in order to achieve valid results. If it was wheat, all breads, cereals, pastas, and many products using starch as fillers (including coffee) must be carefully avoided.

We can often offer substitutes for all eliminated products because there is no one perfect food and no food for which a substitute cannot be found. For example, if a child is taken off milk products, it is possible to supplement the diet with calcium. However, to begin with, we try to manage with as few substitutes as possible.

It is always crucial that a doctor make the decision to eliminate a food on the basis of both history and lab results so that proper vitamin and mineral supplements may be prescribed when necessary.

Childhood illnesses. These are an important part of the medical history. Illnesses may reflect good or poor overall health. They may also indicate foods that should be eliminated. If an infant suffered with many colds and respiratory difficulties, for example, and orange juice was given to "help" but instead further aggravated these conditions, the possibility that the child developed a sensitivity to citrus fruits exists, and therefore these fruits ought to be eliminated from the diet. Another example would be milk, which some children are allergic to, despite the fact it is a healthy food for most.

Sleeping habits. These are checked because, again, children who are uncomfortable will not sleep. We look for some particular pattern of feeding that perhaps contributes to sleeplessness or restless sleeping habits. If a child has an allergy or sensitivity to certain foods, this can cause nervousness, stress, hyperactivity, and other factors that in turn cause wakefulness.

Vitamin supplementation and medications used. Vitamin supplementation is questioned because in certain cases excesses of certain vitamins have been known to encourage such problems as bed-wetting. Some varieties of vitamins are high in sugar, starch, artificial colors, and flavors. These must be discontinued if any elimination diet is to be successfully carried out. It is also important to note the amounts of vitamins taken because of the possibilities of overdoing one vitamin and developing a dietary deficiency of another vitamin.

Medications taken are also questioned. Certain medications may reduce or stimulate appetite and growth curves or may have side effects such as joint pain, deafness, and itching.

Obviously, we do not want to blame food allergies for every complaint we find. We realize that there may be other reasons for some of the problems we see.

In evaluating hyperactive and learning disabled children, it is important to do a careful examination of all factors in their history, growth, and development in order to pinpoint contributing causes. Next, a *family history* is gathered, particularly information about disorders that could provide clues for nutrition counseling for the child. Diabetes, thyroid dysfunction, and allergies suffered by other family members may be clues. These problems do run in families and are often transmitted in one of two fashions: (1) hereditarily, via genetic makeup, or (2) nutritionally, via similarly hereditary and habitual feeding patterns. For example, if a mother hates broccoli, the child will more than likely hate it also because he hears his mother's comments. If she does not eat liver, she probably will not cook liver for her child.

Preventive nutritional measures are employed if obesity, anemia, high cholesterol levels (see "Food Sources of Iron" and "For High-cholesterol Problems" at the end of this chapter), or diabetes are found in a family whose child manifests indicators of any of these conditions.

Appetite and feeding habits are considered before we recommend a diet. Diet recommendations must be realistic and take texture and taste into consideration. A child who does not eat foods with a mushy consistency may go hungry on a regimen of boiled chicken, brown rice, and squash. Knowledge of preferred and disliked foods, snacking habits, and methods of preparation and consumption are crucial to planning a diet. These facts are especially important in a diet for a child whose limited intake both in variety and amounts of foods must provide everything for the child's general good health, maintenance, and function.

Clinical examination by the physician will assess the child's symptoms of nutritional deficiencies or excesses as well as normal growth and developmental patterns. Discussions with the child's mother may often divulge additional information. The "cold" the doctor sees portrayed by puffy eyes and black circles may be characteristic of the child's "Monday afternoon face" after celebrating birthday parties and a weekend of eating out rather than eating nutritious meals at home.

Lab tests include blood, urine, and hair tests to discover if there are any disease factors or imbalances in the body.

Urinalysis. The physical and chemical composition of the urine are checked for normal constituents or significant variations.

T_3, T_4, T_7. The thyroid function is checked via these indicators to rule out thyroid-associated complications in energy metabolism.

SMA 12. Blood chemistry is checked, including cholesterol and triglyceride levels, which may require specific dietary changes.

SGPT (serum glutamic-pyruvic transaminase). Liver function in metabolizing proteins is tested before a diet is recommended.

C.B.C. (complete blood count). Blood values including hemoglobin and hematocrit readings are checked.

> *Hemoglobin* is the iron-protein pigment in the red blood cells that carries oxygen to the tissues.

> *Hematocrit* is the percentage of volume occupied by red blood cells exclusive of plasma and other types of cells.

Biochemical measurements may be the most revealing of all methods employed. Blood tests can indicate more than if a child is simply anemic. The most provocative blood test is the glucose tolerance test (GTT). The GTT tests the ability of the body to handle a known amount of glucose (sugar) used in the blood over a three- to five-hour period. A normal GTT would show a rise in blood sugar one half hour to one hour after ingestion of the glucose and a return to normal level within two to three hours. The blood should never move more than fifty to sixty points within a half hour or drop lower than fasting level by more than fifteen to twenty points.

In a study of 276 children, NYICD reported deviations from the normal GTT in more than 73 per cent of the group.[6] Of these, about 50 per cent showed no elevation of the blood sugar at all, and the remainder of the children showed abnormally high elevations with slow returns to normal or low blood sugars at unusual periods during the test.

This study is highly significant because it is the first such study made anywhere in the world on such a large sample of hyperactive–learning disabled children. A summary of the GTT results for blood samples taken at specific intervals is seen in Figures 1 to 5. Lower than normal values predominated, although some individuals showed a higher than normal response.

The GTT data were also studied in terms of the response curve as a whole. Data were adequate for this in 261 cases, and 26 per cent of those curves showed abnormalities. Figure 1 shows a normal GTT curve. The most frequently observed abnormal curves are illustrated in Figures 2 to 5. (See the Appendix for further details.)

A causal relationship has not yet been definitely identified, but at quick rises or very low drops of blood sugar levels, additional stress is introduced, and the child may encounter great difficulty in keeping awake in class. The erratic changes in blood sugar levels may be directly correlated to erratic ups and downs in behavior and are manifested in mood swings, as seen in the children treated at NYICD. This means that the child's body is not properly fueled and consequently reacts accordingly. Such behavior may cause frequent headaches or a lack of the energetic feeling a child should normally have. These reactions are most noticeable three or four hours after breakfast and at arrival home after long sessions in class.

Correlations between visual problems and erratic blood levels have been made in diabetic adults. Research in the area of learning disabled youth and their visual disorders and GTT curves is needed.

We have already mentioned the probability of allergies that cause physical discomfort and thereby disrupt learning processes. The eosinophil count, a differential value in the complete blood count, if elevated, may be an indicator of infection in the blood by parasites. For instance, in the condition of trichinosis (pork worm) the eosinophil count may go as high as 25 to 50 per cent of white blood cells. In our experience, the eosinophil count is a useful tool in evaluating allergies because it is abnormally high when allergies are present. A possible explanation for this is that

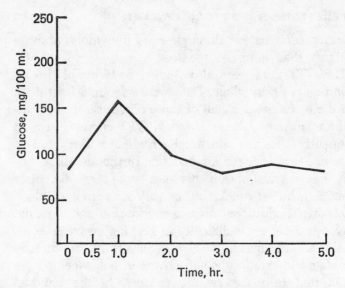

FIGURE 1. *Normal glucose tolerance test curve.*

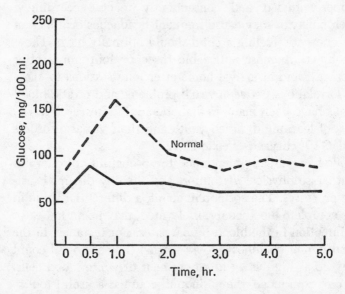

FIGURE 2. *Glucose tolerance test curve characterized by low flat response.*

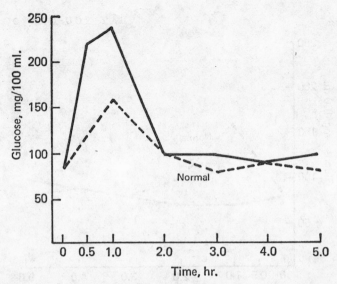

FIGURE 3. *Glucose tolerance test curve with excessive peak and rapid decline.*

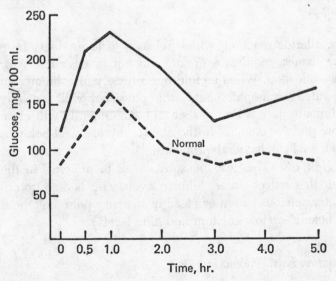

FIGURE 4. *Glucose tolerance test curve with excessive peak and slow recovery.*

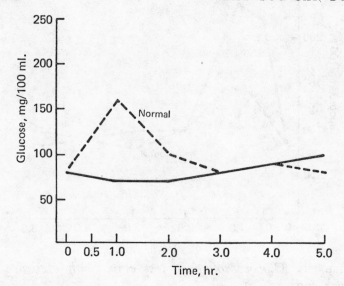

FIGURE 5. *Glucose tolerance test curve with half-moon shape.*

the allergic reaction, which releases toxic products from the tissues, requires a greater amount of eosinophils for detoxification. When a child has a history of colic and an elevated eosinophil count, the physician will probably eliminate milk from the diet and subsequently will often note positive changes in the child's physical well-being as well as in behavioral problems.

Hair test. This test measures levels of minerals in the hair that reflect stored cellular levels. This is done to detect suspicious toxicities (lead or mercury poisoning) and deficiencies (low calcium and zinc levels).

NUTRITIONAL PROGRAM

Once the nutritional problems are identified, what then? First, we provide a few guidelines. The New York

Institute always aims for nutritionally adequate diets for the children. Hyperactive children, like other growing children, need to be fed. The basic diet that we recommend is high in protein and low in carbohydrates, eliminates concentrated sweets, and encourages daily consumption of a variety of foods.

Diet control can play an important role in regulating sugar levels and therefore can aid the child in sitting still and paying attention without his characteristic fidgeting. These children need to be fed between breakfast, lunch, and dinner. Foods high in protein, which are more slowly digested than carbohydrates (because of complexity of structure and high molecular weight), can stabilize blood sugar levels. Proteins are better foods than carbohydrates, and a high-protein diet makes good sense in terms of fostering better behavior and learning possibilities. A consistent supply of glucose to the brain maintains better brain cell function and proteins do this more efficiently.

Small meals of complex carbohydrates (those that are digested more slowly than sweets, including rice; potatoes; whole-grain breads, cereals, and crackers; or fresh fruits and vegetables) together with sources of protein (such as milk, cheeses, yogurt, eggs, lean meats, fish, fowl, nuts, seeds and their butters, dried peas and beans) are the best solutions for simple meals and in-between snacks.

Vitamins and supplements are recommended in several cases:

1. When a child has a particular deficiency or problem noted by the doctor

2. When a child does not or cannot eat particular foods because of allergies or sensitivities and these foods would normally supply a large portion of a particular vitamin requirement

3. When a child needs extra amounts of vitamins and minerals along with a good diet because blood tests indicate subnormal values or because the physician feels that the child needs additional amounts to cope with additional stress

Basic Diet (unless allergies indicate otherwise)

Milk or unflavored yogurt. Two to four cups daily

Protein foods. Poultry, lean meats and fish, cheese, nuts, peanut butter, dried peas and beans, seeds and their butters, five to eight times a day, trusting the child's appetite to determine amounts

Vitamin C source. Orange, grapefruit, tangerine, cantaloupe, tomato juice, and so on, one serving daily

Vitamin A source. Dark green leafy or deep yellow vegetables such as broccoli, carrots, dandelion greens, escarole, spinach, sweet potatoes, one serving daily

Other fruits and vegetables. At least one of each daily

Raw or cooked whole-grain and enriched breads or cereal products. At least four servings daily

Fats. Butter, margarine, or oils, at least two tablespoons daily

Junk Foods

Junk foods with added sugar are eliminated when a sugar metabolism problem is indicated. This may be observed in the GTT test, family history, or if diet records indicate sugar is the major daily consumption. An orange, a food source that is naturally sweet, is all right, but candies and sodas that have sugar added are contraindicated.

Sugar includes white refined sugar, brown sugar, honey, molasses, turbinado sugar, maple syrup, and jelly. Honey is a better food than white sugar because a small amount of trace minerals is found in honey, but it is digested too quickly and in certain cases replaces more important foods needed by the child and is therefore to be avoided. If any of these products are found in foods in large quantities, those foods must not be used, but some products must be allowed so as not to introduce new stress and frustration into the child's life. Ketchup, mayonnaise, most canned and some frozen fruits and vegetables, and store-bought breads have some sugar added in one form or another. These are permissible as long as small amounts are used, and they should always be used in addition to a good basic diet, not instead of it.

Frequent Feedings

We must strive to break people's adherence to the admonitions "Do not eat between meals" and "If you must, take only a raw vegetable or a piece of fruit."

Add more substantial snacks of nuts, cheese and crackers, peanut butter sandwiches, leftover poultry and meat slices (see the "Protein Snacks" list later in this chapter).

The body utilizes many nutrients more effectively in smaller, more frequent feedings, preferably every two or three hours. Therefore, the child will cope better. All this does *not* mean that mother's place is in the kitchen. Absolutely not! The suggested foods can be kept on hand, and the child can help himself. Somehow children manage to help themselves to candy and soda; they do not wait to be served. The same hand will manage to reach for nutritious snack foods if junk foods are not available.

Food Sensitivities

It takes patient children and the whole professional team to determine food sensitivities. The system usually tried is to eliminate suspected foods from the diet for at least ten days to two weeks. The foods are then reintroduced one at a time in small amounts, with a wait of at least three or four days between each food reintroduction.

It might be helpful to keep a diary of food intake and reactions such as irritability, sneezing, fatigue, stomachaches, along with any life situations that might be stressful. This should help to pinpoint any offending foods. Do not attempt this process when the child has a cold or other illness.

Additives

Artificial colors and flavors, BHA, BHT, and salicylates (see the list "Eliminating Salicylates" later in this chapter) are tested by the same kind of elimination procedure used for foods. In many cases we eliminate most of the artificial additives by eliminating sweets because these are the products most likely to be artificially colored and flavored.

Professional Diagnosis

It is most important to use professional help to assess your child's needs. Again, any diet should be recommended only after a complete blood work-up, family and medical histories, and analysis of existing diet have been completed. Otherwise you may cause new problems. A physician's differential diagnosis is always crucial because a professional medical examination can discover facts not considered by the patient. This means not operating on assumptions but using all appropriate medical testing to determine causes. Before recommending a therapeutic diet, we must be sure we will not introduce new problems or unintentionally complicate existing problems for the child.

By employing the use of laboratory tests, medical histories, and diet analysis, we hope to instill good basic nutrition habits and attempt some therapeutic measures as well as to effect more favorable GTT curves, to lower cholesterol, and to raise hematocrit levels (as explained previously).

Analysis of a diet record enables planning of a viable diet, one that will enable the nutritionist and patient to fulfill requirements and that will enable the patient to feel well. The dietary recommendations will be of benefit to the health of the whole family. In all fairness this diet *should* be a family affair, with exceptions, of course, for individual allergies. You may find you are all able to function and cope better with the stresses of living. With everyone on the diet the child will be offered the additional support and encouragement that he needs. We do not wish to institute any new stress regarding the diet. We offer menus and recipes and make the diet easy to follow, inexpensive, and as simple as possible. Note that some children may have a sensitivity to a specific food listed and that the menu or recipe should be altered accordingly.

Here are some useful recommendations for a child who is on a high-protein, low-carbohydrate diet and needs between-meal snacks.

PROTEIN SNACKS

1. Choose one from List A and one from List B so that there is always a source of protein with a source of carbohydrates. Serve in equal amounts.

List A	List B
Potato sticks (no additives)	Walnuts
Pretzels (whole wheat)	Peanuts
Popcorn (no additives)	Sunflower seeds
Raisins	Pumpkin seeds
Celery	Soy nuts
Carrot sticks	

2. Celery stuffed with cottage cheese

3. Celery stuffed with peanut butter

4. Peanut butter and whole-grain crackers

5. Sliced bananas and peanut butter on whole-grain crackers

6. Cheese and crackers

7. Milkshake
    2 cups milk
    ½ cup banana, mashed
    ¼ cup pineapple juice
    ½ cup chopped ice
    Whip ingredients in blender, and serve.

8. Fruit sherbet
    1 egg, beaten
    3 ounces frozen orange juice, unsweetened
    ½ cup water
    ½ cup milk
    Beat ingredients together. Pour mixture into ice trays, and freeze it.

9. Bean dip
    2 cups chick peas
    3 cloves garlic, chopped fine
    1 teaspoon salt
    ½ cup lemon juice
    1 tablespoon olive oil
    Puree chick peas in blender. Add chopped garlic. Combine all ingredients together, and blend.

10. Scoop of salad (such as tuna, egg, or chicken) on whole-grain cracker

11. 1 fried chicken drumstick or wing

12. 1 cheeseburger and tomato wedges

13. 1 slice pizza with whole wheat crust

14. 1 slice whole wheat toast with cottage cheese, raisins, and cinnamon, broiled until brown and bubbling

15. Sardines and whole-grain crackers

16. Cottage cheese–onion dip with pretzels, chips, or raw vegetables

17. 1 cup yogurt (plain) with sliced bananas or pineapple (crushed in its own juice)

18. Fish sticks and tomato juice

19. V-8 juice with brewers' yeast (1 teaspoon)

20. Stuffed pepper (stuffed with chicken salad, tuna salad, or the like)

21. All-natural hot dog and french fries

22. A few meatballs and carrot sticks

23. 1 hard-cooked egg and raw broccoli

MRS. HATCH'S APPLE PIE

CRUST: 2 cups whole wheat flour
         ¾ teaspoon salt
         ½ cup vegetable oil
         ¼–½ cup cold water

Combine the ingredients, and roll out the crust between sheets of waxed paper.

FILLING: 6 apples (McIntosh)
          6½ ounces unsweetened pineapple juice
          1 tablespoon cornstarch
          ¼ teaspoon cinnamon
          ½ teaspoon vanilla
          1½ tablespoons butter

Preheat oven to 350 degrees F. Peel and slice apples into

the pineapple juice. Pour off the juice after coating the apples well. Combine cornstarch, cinnamon, and vanilla in a bowl with the apples. Transfer the mixture to the unbaked pie shell, and dot with butter. Bake for 45 minutes.

ELIMINATING SALICYLATES

The following fruits and vegetables are to be eliminated from the diet in any and all forms. They all contain a chemical compound called salicylic acid. This is a naturally occurring compound and for most people poses no problem; however, it has been our experience that a few children who have behavioral or learning problems have a sensitivity to salicylic acid that may be a causative or aggravating factor in their problems.

Almonds
Apples (juice, cider vinegar,* and so on)
Berries
    blackberries
    boysenberries
    gooseberries
    raspberries
    strawberries
Cherries
Cucumbers (pickle, pickle relish, and so on)
Currants
Grapes and raisins (wine, wine vinegar,* jellies, and so on)
Nectarines
Oranges (Note: grapefruit, lemon, and lime *are* permitted)
Peaches
Plums and prunes
Tomatoes

* Note: Distilled white vinegar may be used.

FOOD SOURCES OF IRON

Lean meats and liver
Dried fruits (e.g., raisins)
Deep green leafy vegetables (e.g., spinach)
Whole-grain breads and cereal products (e.g., wheat
    germ)

FOR HIGH-CHOLESTEROL PROBLEMS

Decrease	*Increase*
Whole milk, butter, cream, cheese, and egg yolks	Skimmed milk and skimmed milk products
Liver, brains, sweetbreads, fish roe, and fatty meats	Lean meats and fish (e.g., chicken, halibut)
	Vegetable oils

Substitute: Fruits and low-calorie desserts for high-fat
    desserts

NOTES

[1] Lillian Langseth and Judith Dowd, "Glucose Tolerance and Hyperkinesis," *Food and Cosmetic Toxicology* 16 (August 1977): 129–133.

[2] The study by F. Monkeberg et al. is cited in N. S. Schrimshaw and J. E. Gordon, eds., "Effect of Early Marasmic Malnutrition on Subsequent Physical and Psychological Development," *Malnutrition, Learning, and Behavior* (Cambridge, Mass.: MIT Press, 1968).

[3] Schrimshaw and Gordon, "Effect of Early Marasmic Malnutrition on Subsequent Physical and Psychological Development."

[4] U. S. Public Health Service, *Ten-State Nutrition Survey, 1968–1970,* DHEW PUB No. (HSM) 72-8134 (Washington, D.C.: U. S. Government Printing Office, 1972).

[5] New York Institute for Child Development Conference, 1976.

[6] Langseth and Dowd, "Glucose Tolerance and Hyperkinesis."

FOOD AND NUTRITION BOARD, NATIONAL ACADEMY OF SCIENCES–NATIONAL RESEARCH COUNCIL RECOMMENDED DAILY DIETARY ALLOWANCES,[a]
Revised 1974

	Age (years)	Weight (kg)	(lbs)	Height (cm)	(in)	Energy (kcal)[b]	Protein (g)	Fat-Soluble Vitamins Vitamin A Activity (RE)[c]	(IU)	Vitamin D (IU)	Vitamin E Activity[e] (IU)
Infants	0.0–0.5	6	14	60	24	kg X 117	kg X 2.2	420[d]	1,400	400	4
	0.5–1.0	9	20	71	28	kg X 108	kg X 2.0	400	2,000	400	5
Children	1–3	13	28	86	34	1,300	23	400	2,000	400	7
	4–6	20	44	110	44	1,800	30	500	2,500	400	9
	7–10	30	66	135	54	2,400	36	700	3,300	400	10
Males	11–14	44	97	158	63	2,800	44	1,000	5,000	400	12
	15–18	61	134	172	69	3,000	54	1,000	5,000	400	15
	19–22	67	147	172	69	3,000	54	1,000	5,000	400	15
	23–50	70	154	172	69	2,700	56	1,000	5,000		15
	51+	70	154	172	69	2,400	56	1,000	5,000		15
Females	11–14	44	97	155	62	2,400	44	800	4,000	400	12
	15–18	54	119	162	65	2,100	48	800	4,000	400	12
	19–22	58	128	162	65	2,100	46	800	4,000	400	12
	23–50	58	128	162	65	2,000	46	800	4,000		12
	51+	58	128	162	65	1,800	46	800	4,000		12
Pregnant						+300	+30	1,000	5,000	400	15
Lactating						+500	+20	1,200	6,000	400	15

[a] The allowances are intended to provide for individual variations among most normal persons as they live in the United States under usual environmental stresses. Diets should be based on a variety of common foods in order to provide other nutrients for which human requirements have been less well defined.

[b] Kilojoules (k J) = 4.2 X kcal.

[c] Retinol equivalents.

[d] Assumed to be all as retinol in milk during the first six months of life. All subsequent intakes are assumed to be half as retinol and half as β-carotene when calculated from international units. As retinol equivalents, three fourths are as retinol and one fourth as β-carotene.

Designed for the maintenance of good nutrition of practically all healthy people in the U.S.A.

Water-Soluble Vitamins							Minerals					
Ascorbic Acid (mg)	Folacin f (µg)	Niacin g (mg)	Riboflavin (mg)	Thiamin (mg)	Vitamin B$_6$ (mg)	Vitamin B$_{12}$ (µg)	Calcium (mg)	Phosphorus (mg)	Iodine (µg)	Iron (mg)	Magnesium (mg)	Zinc (mg)
35	50	5	0.4	0.3	0.3	0.3	360	240	35	10	60	3
35	50	8	0.6	0.5	0.4	0.3	540	400	45	15	70	5
40	100	9	0.8	0.7	0.6	1.0	800	800	60	15	150	10
40	200	12	1.1	0.9	0.9	1.5	800	800	80	10	200	10
40	300	16	1.2	1.2	1.2	2.0	800	800	110	10	250	10
45	400	18	1.5	1.4	1.6	3.0	1,200	1,200	130	18	350	15
45	400	20	1.8	1.5	2.0	3.0	1,200	1,200	150	18	400	15
45	400	20	1.8	1.5	2.0	3.0	800	800	140	10	350	15
45	400	18	1.6	1.4	2.0	3.0	800	800	130	10	350	15
45	400	16	1.5	1.2	2.0	3.0	800	800	110	10	350	15
45	400	16	1.3	1.2	1.6	3.0	1,200	1,200	115	18	300	15
45	400	14	1.4	1.1	2.0	3.0	1,200	1,200	115	18	300	15
45	400	14	1.4	1.1	2.0	3.0	800	800	100	18	300	15
45	400	13	1.2	1.0	2.0	3.0	800	800	100	18	300	15
45	400	12	1.1	1.0	2.0	3.0	800	800	80	10	300	15
60	800	+2	+0.3	+0.3	2.5	4.0	1,200	1,200	125	18+h	450	20
80	600	+4	+0.5	+0.3	2.5	4.0	1,200	1,200	150	18	450	25

e Total vitamin E activity, estimated to be 80 percent as α-tocopherol and 20 percent other tocopherols.

f The folacin allowances refer to dietary sources as determined by *Lactobacillus casei* assay. Pure forms of folacin may be effective in doses less than one fourth of the recommended dietary allowance.

g Although allowances are expressed as niacin, it is recognized that on the average 1 mg of niacin is derived from each 60 mg of dietary tryptophan.

h This increased requirement cannot be met by ordinary diets; therefore, the use of supplemental iron is recommended.

VII

Putting It All Together

After reading the previous chapters, parents may find it helpful to look at the history of one child who was diagnosed and treated at the New York Institute for Child Development and re-evaluated six months later. This digest of a young learning disabled and hyperactive boy's story illustrates the importance of finding and addressing the causes of his problems. Although we have fictionalized the name, the case is a true one and is in many ways typical of the hyperactive and learning disabled children seen at NYICD.

Most important is the fact that this young boy, who came to us a frustrated, hyperactive child who couldn't read or spell, is now a calm, self-reliant learner.

BACKGROUND

John Doe was ten years and nine months old and in a regular fifth grade placement when he was evaluated at the New York Institute for Child Development on October 18, 1977, because of academic underachievement and behavior problems. Although John's behavior problems had somewhat diminished since his earlier school years, Mrs. Doe described him as fidgety, overactive, easily frustrated, unpredictable, and aggressive. In school, John was inattentive, easily distractible, and unable to finish his work. John needed constant support while doing homework and felt overwhelmed by it before he even began to work. His attention span was very short, and he also had bladder control problems.

John's parents were first aware that he had a problem when, as a toddler, he exhibited unusual clumsiness. At age six he became aggressive, wild, and hard to manage in school. Each year, until grade four, John became increasingly difficult to manage. Psychotherapy was tried for a period of about three years. John also had six months of therapy for a visual disability, without significant results.

During testing John was pleasant and cooperative throughout the session. However, it was noted that he was fidgety and easily distracted by background noise.

In the course of taking his developmental history, we learned that milestones were early, particularly in the speech area. Mrs. Doe recalls being amazed that John was vocalizing at five weeks of age. As a toddler, John fell a lot, experiencing many injuries. Before age two he ate the contents of a bottle of Lomotil, which resulted in two respiratory arrests. Medically John's history was interesting because it included contributing factors that often appear in the histories of children with learning difficulties. He was the product of Rh-incompatible parents (second child). He had had bouts of allergic asthma, allergic rhinitis, allergic dermatitis, celiac disease, hay fever, and urinary tract disorders. John's older brother had low blood sugar, and his maternal grandfather had mild diabetes.

On the father's side there was a history of allergic disorders.

John's laboratory work-up was essentially unremarkable except for his glucose tolerance test. His fasting level was normal, 96 milligrams of glucose per 100 cubic centimeters of blood. A spike to 233 after a half hour was well above normal, and the dramatic 95-point drop to 140 at one hour was excessively sharp.

At the time of the evaluation John was on medication for hay fever. His appetite was described as variable, but he had been on a sweet binge prior to testing. He had difficulty in getting to sleep, was a restless sleeper, and was hard to wake in the morning. On occasions he appeared sensitive to lights at night, such as headlights and streetlights.

John's developmental evaluation included assessments of gross, fine, ocular, and basic motor coordination. The speed and efficiency of his performance on the sensorimotor tasks indicated John was able to cope with daily activities without undue stress. Educational testing was also performed to determine the extent to which John's school performance had been affected.

Biochemical assessments, diet analysis, and nutritional evaluations were also performed as part of the dietary work-up.

The following report describes the relationship of each aspect of testing to performance in the classroom and other activities of John's daily life and lists frequently observed symptoms of difficulty:

Nutrition

Undernutrition (deficiency of one or more essential nutrients), overnutrition (excess or imbalance of nutrients), or sensitivity to a specific food or food substance may affect a child's ability to learn, as shown by a short attention span, an inability to concentrate, to sit quietly when necessary, to complete a given task, or to think in an organized manner. Also affected may be a child's behavior pattern, as shown by tantrums, erratic moods, anxieties, or inability to sleep, and a child's physical status, as shown by growth retardation, fatigue, headaches, feelings of weakness, hunger, stomachaches, or bed-wetting.

Dietary assessment: A seven-day diet record (including reactions that might be related to food intake) is completed, and the child's diet is evaluated for adequacy of nutrient intake, amount and sources of carbohydrates, frequency of eating, and any indications of sensitivity or allergic reaction.

John's diet was moderately high in concentrated sweets. It was adequate in milk and dairy products. It was low in servings of protein, including animal and vegetable sources, as well as the frequency of eating these foods. His diet was inadequate in fruits and vegetables, especially fruits high in vitamin A. It was high in refined carbohydrates, and he ate little whole-grain bread and cereal products.

Nutrition consultation: Based on the dietary assessment, medical history, physician's findings, and laboratory reports, a dietary program is planned for the child. The primary goals for every child are to achieve or maintain adequate nutritional intake based on the National Research Council Recommended Daily Dietary Allowances and to avoid concentrated-sugar foods in the diet. The diet is adapted for individual needs, likes, dislikes, sensitivities, and family life-style.

John's diet program called for elimination of all concentrated sweets, along with artificial flavors, colors, and additives. Frequent feedings, to include a source of protein, were to be taken six times daily. Fruits and vegetables, especially good sources of vitamins A and C, were stressed. Whole-grain breads and cereals were to be tried. A diet high in calories was to be used to effect a weight gain. The entire family was to try the diet along with John in order to offer him support and encouragement.

Educational Test Scores

Word Recognition* WRAT Level I	Grade score	4.7
Gates-MacGinitie†	Vocabulary	6.2
Survey D, Form 1	Comprehension	6.1
	Reading speed	4.8
	Reading accuracy	4.9
Gray Oral Reading Test‡ Form A	Grade equivalent	3.4

* *Wide Range Achievement Test (WRAT)*: The WRATs are divided into two levels for ages five to eleven years and twelve years to adulthood. The test measures one's ability to recognize letters and words, to read, to spell, and to do arithmetic calculations. Each part of the test takes between twenty and thirty minutes to administer. The arithmetic test is timed for ten minutes.

† *Gates-MacGinitie Reading Tests:* There are various levels of this test ranging from kindergarten to grade 12. The first four levels of the test consist of two parts: vocabulary and comprehension. The *Vocabulary Subtest* samples the child's ability to recognize or analyze isolated words and to select a synonym. The *Comprehension Subtest* measures ability to read and understand whole sentences and paragraphs. From the fifth level up, an additional subtest is given: *Speed and Accuracy.* This provides an objective measure of how rapidly students can read with understanding. All subtests are timed. Times vary somewhat with the tests themselves.

‡ *Gray Oral Reading Test:* Four forms; primarily used to note types of errors and the relationship of speed to number and types of errors; secondarily used to obtain a grade equivalent for future comparison. Timing is recorded in seconds, and care is needed in recording the beginning and end of each passage. Passages begin at preprimer level and advance to grade 4 and finally adult.

Omissions and insertions of letters were noted in both the word-recognition subtest of the WRAT and the Gray Oral Reading Test. Many substitutions of words were also evident in oral reading. The Slosson Intelligence Test indicated that John was in the superior range (99 percentile).

Sensorimotor Tests

Gross motor ability: Coordinated movements are needed to locate and direct the body in space and are a major factor in maintaining balance. Many visual-performance skills are dependent on gross motor ability. Symptoms of gross motor problems include poor balance and generalized awkwardness.

Various gross motor activities were evaluated, and John's ability was adequate for his age. Balance retrieval was good. Kinesthetic integrity (body awareness) was also satisfactory for his age group.

Fine motor ability: This is the efficient coordination of small-muscle groups in activities directly related to manual skills. Symptoms of difficulty can include poor pencil grasp and inability to tie, button, lace, use scissors, and so on.

Tests of fine motor skills showed that John had inadequate ability to perform rapidly alternating and specific manipulation activities without overflow to the other side of the body. Mrs. Doe reported that John did not tie his shoes well and did not handle scissors well. His pencil grasp was somewhat awkward and stressful, and he exerted heavy pressure during pencil-paper tasks. John tested as right-side dominant.

Eye-hand coordination: Writing and other fine motor tasks can be accomplished quickly and easily only when the eyes work together with the hands. Symptoms of difficulty include poor handwriting; writing neatly but too slowly; drawing with short, sketchy lines; turning paper to draw lines in different directions; inadequate crayoning; and poor execution of ball sports.

Visual-motor function, as measured by the Bender Gestalt Test, was age-appropriate. However, planning and organization were poor, and there were several erasures. John's handwriting indicated difficulty with eye-hand coordination, even though he was able to perform unskilled eye-hand tasks satisfactorily.

Binocularity: This is the ability to use the two eyes together as a team. Symptoms of binocular problems that may be observed or reported are a turned eye, closing or covering one eye, tilting or turning the head in order to use one eye only (specifically when writing), seeing letters and lines run together or words jump, double vision, excessive blinking, gradual loss of reading comprehension, and avoidance of sports involving a ball.

Although John could converge his eyes to the bridge of his nose, stress was observed, and focus was immediately lost. The Keystone Visual Survey Tests indicated a nearpoint convergence problem and poor fusional reserves. Stereopsis (the ability to see in the third dimension) was only 55 per cent. It is interesting to note that John did not participate in typical boys' competitive activities and completely avoided ball sports.

Auditory discrimination: This is the ability to hear and discriminate the difference in sounds. Symptoms of auditory problems may include the need to have directions repeated, inability to master sounds necessary for phonetic skills, poorly modulated voice, and articulation problems.

John was evaluated for auditory discrimination skills (Wepman) and was found to have adequate ability in this area. Auditory memory (Bardel) was in the superior range for his age.

Oculomotor function: This is the ability to control eye movements adequately. Symptoms of inadequate oculomotor function include turning the head (instead of eye movements), omission of words, skipping lines, repetition in reading, use of finger to guide reading, and difficulty copying from the chalkboard.

John's ability to follow a moving object showed inadequate control. Eye movements were jerky on all planes.

Developmental performance: Each child passes through a series of developmental stages. This evaluation determines the child's functional ability at each stage.

John's performance of developmental activities was assessed at the unilateral, bilateral, and spatial orientation levels. John showed poor organization at the bilateral level.

Sensorimotor recommendations: John was given a program of sensorimotor exercises to improve his fine motor, visual, and eye-hand functioning. The program was also designed to establish good binocularity.

Implications: John's coordination difficulties were affecting his ability to perform appropriately without stress in academic areas and prevented him from participating in sports activities. John's function and behavior also appeared to be affected by biochemical imbalances.

John was given sensorimotor and nutrition programs aimed at improving his basic functioning. Our ultimate goals were to allow him to function more efficiently, to modify negative behaviors, and to help him achieve at a level in keeping with his potential.

After monthly visits to the New York Institute for Child Development to monitor and reinforce the program, John was re-evaluated on June 19, 1978.

Educational Test Scores

Word Recognition WRAT Level I	Grade score	5.9
Gates-MacGinitie Survey D, Form 2	Vocabulary	8.0
	Comprehension	9.5
	Reading speed	4.8
	Reading accuracy	4.9
Gray Oral Reading Test Form A	Grade equivalent	2.0

John's reading skills scores generally showed a significant acceleration in growth, particularly in the area of reading comprehension, but his oral reading remained poor. (This skill is the most difficult in which to bring about improvement within a six-month period. The skill is little used or practiced beyond the early grades, and it appears that the integration of oculomotor and auditory function is too challenging for many children with a history of sensorimotor problems. Improvement in oral reading skills is more likely to occur if the child continues on an appropriate exercise program for an additional six months or as long as necessary to consolidate his newly improved sensorimotor skills.)

The functional re-evaluation showed that John had gained adequate control of binocularity, eye-hand coordination, and oculomotor function. He still had some difficulty with fine motor control. John noted improvement in his eye-hand coordination after two months on the program and began participating in ball sports. He still needs special help because he has to catch up with much he had not previously been able to master.

We reap the rewards of helping John when we hear Mrs. Doe's enthusiastic comments about the changes in her son since he was put on the program. Mrs. Doe had tried everything. She had brought her son to doctors, psychiatrists, and other specialists and had about given up until she heard about NYICD. She has told us she feels as though she is living with a new person and now loves her son wholeheartedly, without the resentment, frustration, and guilt feelings that were a constant emotional drain on her.

John has more friends, has leaped ahead incredibly in his schoolwork, and for the first time has made the Little League team. He feels much better about himself because he realizes that he is *not* stupid, clumsy, bad, or dumb. He understands that his body reacts differently to certain things and that that is why he had so many problems and therefore why it is so important for him to stay on the NYICD dietary and exercise program.

VIII

New Law, New Hope

When the Congress enacted Public Law 94-142, the Education for All Handicapped Children Act, which President Ford signed November 28, 1975, there was no sizable reaction from press or public, yet this landmark piece of legislation finally assures the right to education for *all* children.

In the spring of 1977 the first noticeable ripples of interest and questions of implementation began to appear. This did not mean that nothing had been happening, but most of the activity had been going on behind the scenes as the machinery of federal, state, and local government and educational institutions sorted out the ways and means of putting the act in touch with its intended beneficiaries.

In dollars and cents the act is extremely significant. Public Law 94-142 establishes a formula through which the federal government makes a commitment to pay a gradually escalating percentage of the national average expenditures per public school child multiplied by the number of handicapped children being served in the school districts of each state. That percentage will escalate on a yearly basis until 1982, when it will become a permanent 40 per cent each year ($3.16 billion).

One of the most important aspects of the new legislation is the fact that the category of learning disabilities has been included as a handicap *for the first time*. This has posed great problems for federal, state, and local officials. After months of searching in vain for a definition of learning disability, the Bureau of Education for the Handicapped finally posed an interim solution, a formula by which a school might determine whether a child is "severely learning disabled" or not. Although this is not a permanent measure, at least it's a start.

In the future it will be incumbent upon the states and local governments to move with alacrity on the business of learning and translating the law in terms of local needs. This will not be an easy task. The present government estimates of the number of learning disabled children in the country are extremely conservative. We believe that when accurate studies are undertaken from coast to coast, the results will show that at least 15 per cent of the school population will fall into the category of the severely learning disabled.

But the true test of the value of this legislation will come, not in the realization of how many more children are handicapped by learning disabilities, but rather in how successfully those children will be helped to achieve their own potentials. Agencies of government and education must recognize that there are medical and biochemical factors underlying the causes of learning disabilities and that there are medical, nutritional, and sensorimotor therapies that have proved highly effective in restoring learning disabled children to normal classroom function. We are not suggesting that the various techniques now being used by educational specialists are not of value.

However, we believe that these techniques will prove more effective if the physiological sources of many of the problems that handicap the learning disabled child are recognized and taken into consideration.

School systems, their administrators, and special education personnel need to know how they can collaborate with clinics like the New York Institute for Child Development and how they can incorporate the new clinical therapies into the framework of the school curriculum.

UNDERSTANDING PUBLIC LAW 94-142

Public Law 94-142 was signed by President Ford in November 1975. The final regulations were published August 1977, and the law became effective on October 1, 1977. The one section that was not included in the final regulations in August, *Procedures for Evaluating Specific Learning Disabilities*, was published on December 29, 1977.

The life of every learning disabled child in this country will be changed in some way by Public Law 94-142. Because of this, everyone who has any professional contact with children who are, or may be, learning disabled should be acquainted with the law.

The intention of this law is very simple. It stipulates that every learning disabled child is to be given a "free appropriate public education," which means that every child with a specific learning disability is to receive "specially designed instruction and the related services necessary to meet his unique needs."

The regulations that govern the implementation of this law are very long and detailed and will continue to require a great deal of interpretation.

It is essential to remember that this law established

"legal requirements" with which all schools must comply. These are requirements, not recommendations.

Public Law 94-142 Requirements

1. Specific learning disabilities (SLD) are classified as a "handicapped condition." This means that every child with a specific learning disability has the same rights under the law as any other handicapped child. He is considered to be as handicapped as any child with a physical, mental, or emotional disability or disorder.

2. All children with SLD must be identified. "Child counts" are required of local school districts and state education departments by the federal government. Funding will be based on these figures.

3. All children with SLD must be evaluated. A full, fair, and individual evaluation must be conducted for all children who are, or may be, learning disabled. Detailed procedures are included in the regulations that were published on December 29, 1977.

4. Early identification of children with SLD is required, which means that screenings and assessments must be done as early as possible in a child's school career. To encourage identification of preschool-age children with learning problems, the federal government is giving special incentive grants of $300 per child to states for special education and related service programs for handicapped children three years to five years old.

5. A written Individualized Education Program (IEP) must be prepared for each SLD child annually. This means that a specific written plan will have to be developed and implemented for each child.

6. Schools must provide the special education and related services to meet the unique needs of an SLD child. This is *required*, not recommended, and lack of funds is not a sufficient reason for failure to comply.

7. The parents of a child with SLD are guaranteed a free appropriate public education for their child. The parents have extensive rights, and specific procedures are included in the regulations to ensure that these rights are protected.

8. State education departments must help schools meet their responsibility to the SLD child. The federal government is holding each state education department responsible for the implementation of this law, and all states have been preparing themselves to meet their responsibilities. They have developed procedures needed to comply with Public Law 94-142.

9. Federal funds will be provided to help pay for the special education of an SLD child. The level of funding is not yet adequate to provide most districts with the money they need to implement this law, but a specific plan for increasing federal funds every year is included in the regulations.

The requirement that "all children with specific learning disabilities must be identified" brings up the primary question of how this will be done. Professionals must ask themselves the following questions about learning disabled children:

Do I have a child in my class or who has been referred to me who is having difficulty in understanding or using *written* or *spoken* language?

More specifically does this child have trouble performing any of the following functions?
    understanding what he hears
    thinking
    expressing himself orally
    reading
    expressing himself in writing
    doing math

Is there a discrepancy between his ability and his achievement? More specifically, is there a severe discrepancy between his academic achievement and his intellectual ability in one or more of the following areas?

oral expression
listening comprehension
written expression
basic reading skills
reading comprehension
mathematical calculation
mathematical reasoning

If the answer to any of these questions is yes, the child may have a specific learning disability and should be referred to the school official who is responsible for identifying and evaluating handicapped children.

The following conditions are also included in the definition of a specific learning disability: perceptual handicaps, brain injury, minimal brain dysfunction, dyslexia, and developmental aphasia.

If there is any indication of a visual handicap, hearing handicap, or motor handicap, or if there is any indication that the child is mentally retarded, emotionally disturbed, or environmentally, culturally, or economically disadvantaged, the child is not to be identified as a child with SLD. Rather, such a child should be referred to the school official who is responsible for identifying and evaluating handicapped children.

Parents' Rights

After the initial identification and referral an evaluation must be conducted. The law is very specific about the procedures that must be used. But before anything further is done, the parents must be notified and fully informed that their child is being considered for evaluation of his learning problems, and they must be informed of their rights under the law. The parents' rights are a very important feature of Public Law 94-142. Many parents are already aware of these rights and have exercised them or are prepared to do so.

In order to review these rights, assume that you are the parent of a boy, Tommy, who may be learning disabled. Here are a series of questions and answers that are designed to help you understand what your rights are under this law.

1. Can you examine Tommy's records?........Yes
2. Can you request a complete evaluation for Tommy if you think he may be learning disabled?...................................Yes
3. Can you request that an appropriate special education program and related services be provided if the evaluation indicates that he has SLD?..Yes
4. Is the school required to notify you in writing and include an explanation of their decision if they refuse to do an evaluation or if they refuse to provide the special education and related services that have been requested?.................Yes
5. Is the school required to notify you and obtain your consent before Tommy is evaluated?....Yes
6. If you disagree with the evaluation conducted by the school, can you obtain an "independent educational evaluation" for Tommy at public expense?...................................Yes
7. Can you initiate a formal complaint if you are dissatisfied with the evaluation conducted by the school or with the provisions that are being made for Tommy's education?...................Yes
8. Are you entitled to a hearing in connection with your complaint?..........................Yes

9. Can the school use one of its administrators for the hearing officer? . . . . No

10. Who can you take to the hearing to assist you? . . Legal counsel and individuals with specific knowledge or training with respect to the problems of handicapped children.

11. What can you do at a hearing? . . . . Present evidence, confront, cross-examine, and compel the attendance of witnesses.

12. What are you entitled to after the hearing? . . . . A written statement of findings and decisions; a written or electronic verbatim record of the hearing.

13. What can you do if you are dissatisfied with the decisions made by the state department? . . . . You can take your case to a state court or a U.S. district court.

Evaluation Procedures

The final regulations for these evaluation procedures were published on December 29, 1977, and became effective forty-five days from that date, February 12, 1978.

A team is assembled consisting of the child's regular teacher, a teacher or other specialist with knowledge in the area of suspected disability, and an individual qualified to conduct individual examinations of children with the goal of determining if a child has the characteristics enumerated in the definition of a child with a specific learning disability.

The child is assessed in all areas related to the suspected disability, including, where appropriate, health, vision, hearing, social and emotional status, general intelligence, academic performance, communicative status, and motor abilities. Medical services (for diagnostic or evaluation purposes) must be provided if they are necessary to determine a medically related handicapping condition.

At least one team member other than the child's teacher shall observe the child's academic performance in the regular classroom setting.

The team must then prepare a written report of the results of the evaluation, including statements of:

whether the child has a specific learning disability
the basis for the determination
the relevant behavior noted during the observation
the relationship of the behavior to the child's academic functioning
the educationally relevant medical findings
whether there is a severe discrepancy between achievement and ability that is not correctable without special education and related services
the effects of environmental, cultural, or economic disadvantages

If it is determined that the child has a specific learning disability and needs "special education and related services," an IEP must be prepared. What happens to the child will be determined by the contents of his IEP. It will define his instructional program, which the law stipulates is to be "specifically designed to meet his unique needs," and it will specify which "related service(s)" he is to receive. Related services are defined under the law and include almost any type of developmental, corrective, or other supportive service that the child will need to benefit from his special education.

The IEP is a written statement developed in a meeting that must include the following participants: the child's teacher, a representative of the local school district who is qualified to provide or supervise the provision of instruction specially designed to meet the needs of handicapped

children, the parents, the child (where appropriate), and
other individuals at the discretion of the parents or
school.

The IEP must include the following information: present educational levels; annual goals; short-term instructional objectives; services to be provided, including dates
of their initiation and anticipated duration; objective cri-
teria for evaluation; and evaluation procedures. The IEP
must be established or revised at the beginning of each
school year or within thirty days of the determination
that the child needs "special education and related services."

A Final Note

Parents seeking information on where to get help for
their child often contact the New York Institute. The best
advice we can offer is to write to these agencies:

Association for Children with Learning Disabilities
(ACLD)
4156 Library Road
Pittsburgh, Pennsylvania 15234

(You can also write to the local chapter of ACLD in your
area. The national chapter will send you their address
upon request.)

Council for Exceptional Children
1920 Association Drive
Reston, Virginia 22091

Closer Look
Box 1492
Washington, D.C. 20013

Academic Therapies Publications
20 Commercial Boulevard
Novato, California 94947

(You may write for their *Directory of Educational Facilities for the Learning Disabled*)

The New York Institute for Child Development, Inc.
205 Lexington Avenue
New York, New York 10016

Glossary

This glossary includes some terms that are not used in the book but that may be used by schools or professionals in relation to the learning disabled child.

A

ABILITY GROUPING Bringing together children at the same achievement level (or with similar potential) for purposes of instruction.

ABILITY TEST An examination purported to measure a child's educational potential; also an IQ test.

ACCELERATION Advancing a child beyond the normal grade level for his age; also called *skipping*.

ACCOMMODATION The process by which structures within the eyes change their shape to bring an object into focus on the retina at varying distances.

ACHIEVEMENT The degree to which a child assimilates learning tasks presented in the classroom.

ACHIEVEMENT TEST A device used to measure how much a child has learned of what has been taught.

ACTING OUT Reacting to stress physically, rather than by talking out the problem.

AFFECTIVE Pertaining to the emotional aspects of human behavior.

ALEXIA Loss or impairment of the ability to understand written language; also called *word blindness*. (See DYSLEXIA)

ALLERGY Altered response of cells to a substance (usually a protein contained in drugs, pollens, molds, lints, animal danders, dandruff, cosmetics, industrial chemicals, and so on), resulting in a variety of manifestations such as eczema, fatigue, cough, nasal congestion, irritability.

AMBLYOPIA The tendency for the eye(s) to wander because of a muscular imbalance; also called *lazy eye*.

AMINO ACIDS Organic compounds containing nitrogen, known as the building block of the protein molecule.

ANTECEDENT What occurs just prior to and causes a particular behavior.

APHASIA The loss or impairment of the ability to understand or communicate language, either spoken or written. In children aphasia is characterized by an inability to label familiar objects. Instead of "pot," for example, the aphasic child will say, "That thing you cook things in."

AVITAMINOSIS Condition caused by the lack of a vitamin in the diet or by lack of absorption or utilization of it.

ARTICULATION The action of the tongue, teeth, and lips as they interrupt the tone produced by the vocal cords during speech (refers especially to consonant sounds).

AUDITORY DISCRIMINATION The ability to tell differences between sounds.

AUDITORY MEMORY The ability to store and accurately recall the spoken word.

AUDITORY PERCEPTION The accuracy with which the sound striking the eardrum is interpreted by the brain.

AUDITORY SEQUENCING The ability to repeat accurately a series of uttered sounds or words.

AUTISM Immersion in a world of fantasy to the complete or partial exclusion of reality, characterized by noncommunication.

B

BASIC SKILLS The kinds of learning (recognition of colors, sizes, shapes, and positions; fine motor abilities) considered necessary to begin formal education.

BEHAVIOR MODIFICATION A technique in which conditioning is used to attain desired behaviors. (See REINFORCEMENT, CONDITIONING)

BILINGUAL/BICULTURAL EDUCATION An instructional program designed to teach a child of two different language and cultural backgrounds the languages and cultures of both.

BINOCULAR The use of two eyes at the same time.

C

CEREBRAL CORTEX The surface layer of the brain; the primary controlling agent of an individual's psychological functions.

CHOLINE Component of lecithin necessary for fat transport in the body; prevents accumulation of fat in the liver.

CHRONOLOGICAL AGE (CA) The age of an individual expressed as years, months, and days.

COGNITIVE Pertaining to ideas or thoughts.

COLOR BLINDNESS The inability to distinguish colors. (The term now in use is *color deficiency*.)

CONDITIONING Obtaining a behavior that has never occurred before by pairing it with a behavior that normally occurs. (The Russian physiologist Pavlov conditioned a dog to salivate at the sound of a bell by ringing it each time the dog was given food.)

CONFLICT RESOLUTION A method of guiding children in an examination of nonviolent alternatives for dealing with anger.

CONSEQUENCE An event that occurs following a behavior; may be a natural event (being burned by touching a hot stove) or artificial (being deprived of viewing TV for failing to carry out a responsibility).

CONVERGENCE The ability to make both eyes focus on a single object. This should occur anywhere from the nose to the horizon.

CORTICAL OPPOSITION Uniquely human ability to oppose the tip of the thumb to the tip of the index finger; necessary for correct pencil holding, tying, and so on.

CRAWLING First true forward movement, with abdomen on the floor. (Patterns of movement on the floor usually progress from homologous to homolateral to bilateral.)

CREATIVITY Searching for and finding new relationships between concepts and new solutions to problems.

CREEPING Moving forward on hands and knees.

CRITERION REFERENCED Matching an established standard of performance. (See PERFORMANCE OBJECTIVE)

CROSS-PATTERN WALKING Structured walking is an exercise that facilitates the easy gait of natural cross-pattern walking.

CURSIVE Writing in which the letters are joined.

D

DECIBEL A measure of the loudness of sound; also used to describe the degree of hearing loss.

DIAGNOSTIC-PRESCRIPTIVE TEACHING An approach that uses an ongoing teaching-testing-teaching process. First the strengths and weaknesses of the individual are analyzed; then specific objectives are designed to correct the deficiencies.

DIFFERENTIAL DIAGNOSIS Finding out not only what the problem is but also where it is. (A differential diagnosis would indicate, for example, whether a child's visual problem is cortical, midbrain, or pons level.)

DIPLOPIA One object appears as two; double vision.

DIRECTIONALITY Discrimination of the positions of objects at first relative to one's self and then, at a later stage of development, relative to one another. This skill is necessary for reading and writing.

DISCIPLINE Self-control or the teaching of self-control.

DISTRACTIBILITY The inability to attend to incoming information that is pertinent to the solution of the problem at hand; the inability to keep one's mind on a task.

DYSLEXIA The inability to deal with or decode printed symbols; may affect reading, writing, and/or spelling.

E

EARLY CHILDHOOD EDUCATION (ECE) Specifically a program designed to ensure the successful completion of kindergarten to third grade by identifying areas of weakness and providing special assistance.

EDUCATIONALLY HANDICAPPED (EH) See MINIMAL BRAIN DYSFUNCTION and LEARNING DISABILITY.

EGO The self; the core of one's personality.

EMOTIONAL BLOCK Temporary impairment of learning ability as a result of stress (e.g., frustration, anxiety, pressure).

EMPATHY An awareness of how another person is reacting emotionally; a vicarious participation in those emotions.

EMPIRICAL Obtained through actual observation.

ENURESIS Bed-wetting.

EOSINOPHIL A white blood cell (sensitive to the dye eosin) the level of which is elevated in the presence of stress, allergies, or parasites. (A count of 0 to 3 is normal.)

ESL English as a second language; a means of helping non-English-speaking students to adjust to standard classroom English.

EXPERIENCE APPROACH A reading instruction method that uses a child's own experiences. He tells something of importance to him, and it is typed and read to or by him.

EYE-HAND COORDINATION The movement of the hand in conjunction with and under the control of the eyes. (At first the child's eyes follow his hand.)

F

FAST LEARNER One who is able to acquire skills or knowledge at a significantly faster rate than others.

FINE MOTOR Pertaining to the use of small muscles, such as those of the fingers and eyes. (See GROSS MOTOR)

FROSTIG Test and/or materials for training visual perception designed by Dr. Marianne Frostig.

FRUCTOSE Sugar found in fruits and honey; also called *levulose*.

FUSION The ability of the brain to fuse the images perceived by both eyes into one image.

FUSIONAL RESERVE Amount of stress the eyes can tolerate before double vision occurs.

G

GESTALT The perception of an object as a whole or a unit. (A square, for example, is viewed in its totality, not as four straight lines of equal lengths at right angles to each other.)

GIFTED Intellectual achievement that places a person at the top 2 per cent of all those measured; an IQ of around 130. (See IQ)

GLUCOSE Sugar found in fruits and honey; blood sugar; also known as *dextrose*.

GNOSTIC SENSATION Sense of light touch and temperature.

GRADE EQUIVALENT SCORE An achievement test score that is expressed in terms of school year and month. (A score of 3.8, for example, means achievement equal to that expected at the eighth month of the third grade.

GROSS MOTOR Refers to the large muscles, such as those controlling the arms and the neck. (See FINE MOTOR)

H

HALO EFFECT The tendency for one behavior to influence the attitude of an observer, so that he or she rates other behaviors of the same individual accordingly. (E.g., the child whose work is neat tends to get better grades than a child of similar ability whose work is sloppy.)

HANDEDNESS Being predominantly right-handed or left-handed. (Handedness usually develops around the second year of life.)

HEALTH FOOD A food that contributes to the proper growth and development of the body.

HOMOLOGOUS Movement of upper limbs together followed by lower limbs (e.g., bunny hop).

HOMOLATERAL Alternate movement of arm and leg on the same side of the body.

HYPERACTIVITY Excessive or exaggerated muscular activity; also called *hyperkinesis* (*hyper*, "increased," *kinesis*, "motion").

HYPERVITAMINOSIS Condition caused by an excess of one or more vitamins.

HYPOACTIVE Decreased motor activity; also called *hypokinesis* (*hypo*, "decreased").

HYPOGLYCEMIA Blood sugar level below normal.

I

ILLINOIS TEST OF PSYCHOLINGUISTIC ABILITIES (ITPA) A test designed to measure the ability of the young child (age two and a half to nine) to receive and express language.

IMMATURITY Generally, unreadiness to undertake an educational task or tasks or to profit from a structured educational experience. Reasons may be physical, social, or psychological or some combination of these.

INDIVIDUALIZED INSTRUCTION An educational approach based on each child's readiness level in each subarea of instruction; that is, an approach that deals with individual differences.

INTELLIGENCE QUOTIENT (IQ) The relationship of an individual's mental age (MA) to his or her chronological age (CA); the mental age divided by the chronological age and multiplied by 100. (A mental age of 5 years, 10 months at the chronological age of 5 years, 10 months yields an IQ of 100.)

ISOLATE A child who is excluded from (or excludes himself from) the society of his classmates, schoolmates, or friends; a loner.

K

KETOSIS Accumulation in the body of ketone bodies as a result of incomplete oxidations of the fatty acids.

KINESTHESIS Sense of joint position, weight distribution, and movement. This sense provides us feedback about our body, and it is this that prevents us from falling over our own feet.

L

LABILITY   Instability of emotions.

LANGUAGE ARTS   All aspects of communication, including reading, writing, spelling, speech, listening. Reading is generally accorded a separate designation, that is, "reading and language arts."

LATERALITY   Consistent use of the eye, hand, foot, and ear of one side of the body for skilled acts; reflects the degree of cortical hemisphere dominance.

LEARNING DISABILITY GROUP (LDG)   A small-group instructional arrangement for children who have learning disabilities. Children spend only part of the day in the group setting, as compared with the EH (educationally handicapped) class, which is a self-contained, full-day program.

LOOK-SAY   A method of teaching reading that relies primarily on the visual recognition of words; often incorrectly referred to as the *look-see* method. (See PHONETIC)

M

MANUSCRIPT   Writing that uses printed, unjoined letters. (See CURSIVE)

MASTERY   Successful performance of an educational task at a predetermined level of proficiency.

MEAN   The mathematical average or the total of the scores divided by the number of scores.

MEDIAN   The middle score in a group of scores arranged from high to low or vice versa.

MENTAL AGE (MA)   A measure of mental attainment obtained by testing. (An individual who does as well as the average ten-year-old does on such a test has an MA of ten years.)

MENTALLY RETARDED (MR)   Unable to function at a level commensurate with one's chronological age; unable to conceptualize, having insufficient language development, and demonstrating social skills and behavior that are inappropriate. Two major categories are the educable mentally retarded (EMR) and the trainable mentally retarded (TMR). The former can be educated to varying degrees through the use of special approaches; the latter can be trained to function socially, attend to their personal needs, and work in a sheltered workshop setting. (Retardation is an arbitrary matter; for example, to the extent that you are more intelligent than I, I am retarded.)

METABOLISM   Physical and chemical changes occurring within the organism, including synthesis of biological materials and the breakdown of substances to yield energy.

MINIMAL BRAIN DYSFUNCTION (MBD)   The inability to learn through normal methods in spite of at least average intelligence; also called *educationally handicapped* (EH), *neurologically handicapped* (NH), *specific learning disability* (SLD), *Strauss's syndrome, hyperactive syndrome*, and a number of other terms.

MONOCULAR   The use of one eye.

MULTI-AGE GROUPING   An instructional organization in which children of several different ages are in a single classroom, with each child proceeding at his own pace.

MYELIN   The sheath or covering surrounding nerves and nerve tissue (including the brain) that provides nourishment and facilitates the transmission of impulses.

N

NATURAL FOOD   No technical or legal definition accepted; food grown without synthetic fertilizers or pesticides and/or processed without synthetic additives.

NEUROLOGICAL ORGANIZATION   The process whereby the organism subject to environmental forces achieves the potential inherent in its genetic endowments.

NUTRIENT   Chemical substance in foods that nourishes the body (e.g., amino acid, fat, calcium).

NYSTAGMUS   An involuntary back-and-forth movement of the eyes.

O

OBJECTIVE MEASUREMENT   An evaluation (or scoring) that is supposedly independent of any bias on the part of the person doing the evaluating.

OPEN CLASSROOM In general, a classroom so arranged that the individual child is encouraged to follow his or her own interests. The teacher is a manager and a facilitator of learning.

ORGANIC Any compound containing carbon.

OVERCONVERGENCE A condition in which the two eyes tend to fixate at a point closer than reading distance, therefore requiring great effort to reposition outward.

OVERFLOW Involvement of both sides of the body when the child is asked to perform a fine skill with only one part of his body (e.g., hand).

P

PARALLEL PLAY Describes the tendency of children at about age three or four to play side by side but not really together.

PEER GROUP One's intellectual and/or social and/or educational equals.

PERCENTILE A score that ranks an individual relative to those who fall below or above him. (A score at the fifty-eighth percentile, for example, means that out of every one hundred persons tested, fifty-eight would fall below and forty-two above.)

PERCEPTION The interpretation by the brain of information obtained through the senses.

PERFORMANCE OBJECTIVE An educational task that is described in terms of who will do it, under what conditions, at what time, the standard acceptable, and how attainment will be measured. For instance, a reading objective for a child may be that he or she will learn all the beginning consonants after three weeks of instruction as measured by a test the teacher has devised.

PERSEVERATION The continuance of a behavior after the need for it has passed or when it is no longer appropriate.

PHOBIA An unreasoned fear that produces great anxiety. Usually the victim of a phobia will indulge in an activity that

GLOSSARY   145

permits him to escape what he believes to be the object of
fear. (See SCHOOL ANXIETY)

PHONICS OR PHONETICS In general, a reading approach that
focuses primarily on the sounds of words as they relate to
their written representations.

PLATEAU A period of no apparent progress in learning. A
new approach may be necessary, or the child may merely
be getting it all together before going on to the next step.

PREDOMINANT EYE The eye that reflects the dominant cortical
hemisphere as measured by sighting, control, and function.

PREHENSILE GRASP Immature grasp involving either a fisting
motion or a scissor motion of the thumb and index finger.

PROGNOSIS An educated guess (i.e., one based on available
information) concerning the future course of a condition or
situation.

PROJECTIVE TEST A questioning or other information-gather-
ing technique that enables an individual to provide information about his/her personality by projecting himself into
a response. (One well-known projective test, the Rorschach
Test, uses inkblots and asks the individual being tested to
tell the examiner what each inkblot looks like to him/her.)

PSYCHOLINGUISTICS The study of the mental processes underlying the acquisition and use of language.

PSYCHOMETRIST One who is trained to administer psychological tests.

PSYCHOMOTOR Activity involving both physical and psychological aspects.

PURSUITS Tracking a moving object smoothly with both eyes.

R

RAPPORT A relationship characterized by mutual confidence
and cooperation.

READING READINESS The stage of development at which,
under ordinary circumstances, a child is ready to begin
reading. Neurological, psychological, social, emotional, and
other factors must be considered.

REALITY THERAPY A psychiatric approach, developed by Dr.

William Glasser, that, as applied to the classroom, stresses increased involvement of the child in the educational process.

REGRESSION   A retreat to a lower stage of maturity. Regression sometimes occurs when stress threatens the integrity of the ego. (See EGO)

REINFORCEMENT   Experiences and activities designed to support something already taught; also a term used in the behavior modification approach that is known as *operant conditioning*. In this case, reinforcement means immediately following a desired behavior with something (very loosely, a reward) that is likely to cause a repetition of that behavior.

REMEDIAL READING   An approach designed to assist the children who have not acquired one or more of the skills presumed basic to reading readiness or whose basic skills are inadequate; often these are children who were introduced to formal reading instruction before they were ready.

RETENTION   Repetition of a grade in school; also, the ability to memorize.

REVERSAL   The tendency to read or write backward (*was* for *saw*, for example, or *b* for *d*).

RIGHTING REFLEX   Natural bodily reactions to maintain balance.

RITALIN   A trade name for the generic stimulant drug methylphenidate, often prescribed for hyperactivity.

S

SCHOOL PHOBIA   An anxiety that is manifested in fear of school and refusal to attend. (See SEPARATION ANXIETY)

SCHOOL PSYCHOLOGIST   A specialist trained in the administration of objective and projective tests. He or she can measure ability, analyze personality patterns, and provide diagnostic and prescriptive information; in some cases, he or she also provides therapy.

SELF-CONCEPT   One's overall opinion of oneself.

SENSORY   Pertaining to information the individual gains through the senses.

SENSORIMOTOR The interaction between the senses and the muscular system through which the child attains the initial stage in his/her development. (He/she explores by touching, tasting, and so on.)

SENSORIMOTOR THERAPY A system whereby movements are programmed specifically to affect the sensory system, which will then change and reinforce the motor system.

SEPARATION ANXIETY A child's fear of leaving his/her parents (most often his/her mother), for example, to go to school. Separation anxiety is most often behind school phobia. (See SCHOOL PHOBIA)

SIBLING A brother or sister.

SIGHTING EYE The eye we sight with when, for example, using a telescope.

SLOW LEARNER A child who learns more slowly than others.

SNELLEN'S CHART A chart used to test the efficiency of distance vision; it displays letters and symbols of varying and graded sizes.

SOCIOGRAM A chart that shows the interrelationships among the members of a group.

SPECIFIC LEARNING DISABILITY (SLD) See MINIMAL BRAIN DYSFUNCTION.

SPEECH THERAPIST A specialist who is trained to diagnose and treat problems having to do with language development.

STANDARDIZED TEST A test that has been given to enough individuals to provide a scale of performance expectations (e.g., a standard has been established for a particular age or a particular grade level).

STANINE (STANDARD NINE) A score that indicates placement on a nine-point scale; a score of five is the median. (See MEDIAN)

STEREOGNOSIS The tactile ability to identify objects in three dimensions.

STEREOPSIS Three-dimensional vision.

STIMULUS Anything in an individual's environment that can arouse a reaction or response.

STRABISMUS Inability to direct the eyes at the same point simultaneously because of an imbalance of the eye muscle; commonly called *crossed eyes*.

SUBJECTIVE MEASUREMENT A measurement that involves, at least to some extent, the impressions, intuitions, or hunches of the person doing the measuring.

SYNDROME A group of symptoms that are generally found together in a particular disorder and that are typical of that disorder. (The hyperactive syndrome, for example, consists of excessive movement, distractibility, short attention span, perseveration, and perceptual problems.)

T

TELEBINOCULAR A device sometimes used in schools to test for vision problems. (Its use does not constitute an examination.)

TMR See MENTALLY RETARDED.

U

UNDERACHIEVEMENT Educational attainment below one's evidenced ability.

UNDERCONVERGENCE Abnormal difficulty in converging the two eyes so that they easily fixate at a near point.

V

VALUES CLARIFICATION An educational adjunct that exposes children to an examination of their own ideals so that they learn to make choices based on their own value systems.

VESTIBULAR The mechanism(s) situated in the middle and inner ear whose function is regulating all balancing and awareness of the body's position in space and movement through space.

VISUAL ACUITY Sharpness of the image focused on the retina of the eye.

VISUAL, AUDITORY, TACTILE, KINESTHETIC (VATK) A teaching method that simultaneously employs all these learning channels.

VISUAL CLOSURE A tendency of the brain to supply missing

parts from familiar objects. (E.g., a broken circle or a square that has parts of two or three sides missing will nevertheless be perceived as a whole circle or a whole square.

VISUAL MEMORY The ability to recall information that was visually received.

VISUAL-MOTOR A relationship between the eyes and other movement. (Eye-hand coordination is an example of a visual-motor relationship.)

VISUAL PERCEPTION The interpretation by the brain of visually presented information.

VISUAL SEQUENCING The ability to recall in their original order a number of objects that were presented visually.

VITAL SENSATIONS Sense of pain and pressure.

W

WITHDRAWAL Behavior characterized by shyness, overconformity, feelings of inadequacy and unimportance, fear, and anxiety. Often withdrawn children are ignored because they are not seen as having behavior problems. If untreated, withdrawal can become very serious and may lead to childhood schizophrenia.

WORD-CALLING In reading, correctly pronouncing words without comprehending their meaning.

X

XYLOSE A sugar that is not metabolized by the body.

Y

YOKING Both eyes moving together.

Appendix

The predominant abnormality, accounting for 50 per cent of the abnormal GTT results, was a low flat curve (Fig. 2). Fifteen per cent of the curves evidenced abnormally high peaks with extremely rapid declines (Fig. 3), and almost 11 per cent (twenty-one cases) had abnormally high peaks with slow recoveries (Fig. 4). In fifteen of the twenty-one subjects with the latter type of curve, elevated cholesterol levels were also found. Glucose was present in the urine during peak serum glucose levels in thirteen of these twenty-one cases. Almost 11 per cent of the abnormal curves showed a decline immediately after glucose ingestion, with a slow rise in glucose levels and a terminal value higher than fasting values (Fig. 5). Of the remaining 14 per cent of the abnormal curves, 8 per cent were characterized by normal peaks with slow declines and 6 per cent by high peaks or rapid declines. Acetone was not detected in the urine of any of the subjects studied at any time during GTT.

Index